THE FIVE-HUNDRED YEAR BOOK

OF THE

UNIVERSITY OF GLASGOW

1451 — 1951

THE UNIVERSITY

Photo by Fenton Studios

THE
FIVE-HUNDRED YEAR
BOOK

TO COMMEMORATE
THE FIFTH CENTENARY OF
THE UNIVERSITY OF GLASGOW

1451 – 1951

Edited by
IAN R. HAMILTON

Published by
THE STUDENTS' FIFTH CENTENARY COMMITTEE, THE UNIVERSITY, GLASGOW

Printed by

MACKILL & CO. LTD., 86 YORK STREET, GLASGOW, C.2

To the people of Scotland,
the heirs of our inheritance

Do Shluagh na h-Albann
luchd-seilbh ar dìleib

Scotiae Populo
hereditatis nostrae heredibus

CONTENTS

	Page
Foreword - - - - - - -	xiii
The Principal Sir Hector Hetherington, K.B.E., D.L., LL.D., D.LITT.	
Message from the Rector - - - - -	1
John M. MacCormick, LL.B.	
A Historical Sketch of the University - - -	3
Frank W. Provan, M.A.	
The Glasgow Undergraduate - - - -	10
James Bridie	
Glimpses of Science - - - - -	18
Eric Reeves	
Queen Margaret Students' Union - - -	24
Stroma Duncan	
The Rectors and the University - - -	29
Compton Mackenzie, O.B.E., LL.D.	
Town, Gown and Students - - -	38
Charles C. Robson, M.A.	

Page

A G.U.M. Sidelight - - - - - - 46
   Archibald Duncan Thomson

Minute by Minute in the life of the Students'
         Representative Council - - - - 50
   Donald Macmillan.

The Legacy of Five Hundred Years - - - 60
   The Chancellor, Lord Boyd Orr of Brechin,
   D.S.O., M.C., LL.D., F.R.S.

Alma Mater - - - - - - - 64
   Mackhan Dube

The University and Art - - - - - 74
   T. J. Honeyman

The Dialectic Society - - - - - - 82
   James Willocks

The Slide that Jammed - - - - - 91
   Art Student

The Old College - - - - - - 96
   Elspeth Gallie, M.A.

Union Debates - - - - - - 104
   Right Honourable Hector McNeil, M.P.

The Student International Club - - - - 109
   Victor S. Godfrey

Thae Students - - - - - - - 113
   C. A. Oakley, B.SC., ED.B.

	Page
The Union	124
W. G. A. Craig	
The Student in Print	128
I. P. C. Murray	
The Registrar	136
John S. Young	
The Clydeside and the Documentary Film	140
John Grierson, M.A., LL.D.	
Earning Between Learning	150
Alan C. Brown	
Glasgow University Athletic Club	158
W. R. Cunningham, M.A., LL.D.	

ILLUSTRATIONS

Page

The University of Glasgow   -   -   Frontispiece

Queen Margaret Union   -   -   -   Facing Page 27

Pearce Lodge   -   -   -   -   -   -   -   55

The Foulis Academy   -   -   -   -   -   -   77

Slezer's View of the Old College -   -   -   -   99

The Union -   -   -   -   -   -   -   -   125

FOREWORD

By The Principal Sir Hector Hetherington,
K.B.E., D.L., LL.D., D.Litt.

It is a truth universally acknowledged that in every cycle of forty or fifty years, a lively society must accomplish a literary revolution. This is called a Revival or a Renaissance or an Aufklarung or a pre-Something or a post-Somebody or, if it be very recherché, a Geometrical Shape. It means that the writers of the current mode think poorly of their recent predecessors, and despite the probabilities, take a more hopeful view of their own chances of survival. This is a just and wholesome attitude of mind. Nobody can invest his writing with even a milligramme of meaning unless he believes that he speaks a new and authentic word to which posterity will lend an attentive ear.

Yet, when you come to look at the story, you find it hard to discover the crises. There is, for example, the present Scottish Renaissance. All instructed persons agree that the whole business really derives from the literary doings of the students of this University in or about the first decade of the present century: and that (with occasional assistance from the authors of the establishments in the East) it has been fostered by the continuous literary exuberance of their successors in this place in every decade since. There is no break at all.

It begins around the time of the Ninth Jubilee. I do not know that the Jubilee had much to do with it. There were other more relevant conditions such as the recent impact on Glasgow of Murray and Phillimore, of Raleigh and Dixon, who as well as being scholars, liked to exercise themselves and others in the practice of letters. And now we come to the Tenth: and to the essential matter of handing on the same seemly craft and habit. To that intent is this volume of the S.R.C.—its Commemoration Volume. Phillimore wrote of the G.U.M. as ' both a Didactic and Recording Muse.' Here is the same duality of purpose— declaring the past, portending what is to be. The contributors? Most have served their stint filling the pages of that cheerful sheet. They make their bow again, under some measure of that editorial duress which they were wont to suffer or to practise: and to the same ends. I hope it may be to the same effect: and that their successors of the Eleventh, though no doubt better men than they, will still discover in their meditations something to think about.

MESSAGE FROM THE RECTOR
JOHN M. MACCORMICK, LL.B.

> On 21st October, 1950, *Glasgow Students made
> University history by electing a local man as Rector.
> The writing of this message was one of the first duties
> of the new Rector.*

The greatest value to us of any human institution is that
it should have grown in an entirely organic fashion, from
embryo to maturity, and that it should display a continuity
in its growth which likens it to a living individual. Its
history thus conveys a sense of inward and intuitive purpose, transcending any conscious plan, and reaching ends
which in the beginning could not have been foreseen. It
is in this way that institutions become living communities;
and it is in membership of a community that the individual
finds his richest personal development.

There can be no better example of such growth of
institutions than the Universities of Europe, among which
our own University of Glasgow holds an ancient and
honourable place. And there is no better way of showing
our indebtedness to our community or our appreciation
of it as a thing which has grown with a life of its own,
than to remember the stages of its development and to
mark the great occasions in its history. That is why in
1951 we celebrate our foundation 500 years ago and thus
enrich the present by paying tribute to the past.

B

I hope that in doing so the whole body of students will find a deeper sense of identity with their Alma Mater. In my own day it was fashionable in certain quarters to deride the idea of the " corporate life " and to regard those students who took any active part in University affairs either as minor place-seekers or as useless busybodies. No doubt critics will be as vocal to-day as they were then and there will be just as many undergraduates who believe that the University has nothing to offer them but examinations and a degree. Such people might as well take correspondence courses as become matriculated students, for they lose the chief advantage that the University has to give them—the advantage of becoming members of a community and drawing strength and wisdom from their fellows.

That the student is still important, not as a pupil only but as a member of a self-governing guild, is proclaimed in his right to elect the Rector. Although the rectorship has become, and in some senses must remain an honorary position, it can still fulfil the function of symbolising the corporate existence of the student body. A University which is in the main non-residential and which enrols over 7,000 students every year tends to become an impersonal place. It is by preserving the best of our traditions and re-interpreting them in the light of modern needs that such impersonality can largely be dispelled. My hope is that during the three years of office as Rector into which I have now entered it may be possible to discover the means of making the Rectorship, which constitutes an almost unique link with the past, a real and useful help in the expression of student aims and ideals in the present.

A HISTORICAL SKETCH OF THE UNIVERSITY

By FRANK W. PROVAN, M.A.

Frank Provan matriculated at the University in 1942. After service in the Royal Navy from 1943 to 1946 he returned to Gilmorehill, edited Ygorra and the G.U.M. and graduated with Honours in Economics. He is now a sub-editor on the staff of the Glasgow Herald.

WHEN Bishop William Turnbull applied for authority to establish a school of higher learning in the See of Glasgow, the resultant Papal Bull recognised the proposed new institution as an addition to the great series of *Studia Generalia* which, since the first half of the twelfth century, had been spreading to countries throughout Europe. The first great medieval schools, Bologna, Paris, and Oxford, had been recognised as *Universitates* or organised groups of scholars between 1140 and 1170, almost a century before they came to possess any corporate buildings or other property, and since the end of the twelfth century the migration of graduates from these schools and the radical ambitions of local nobles and clergy had caused the foundation of universities in centres as wide-spread as Prague and St. Andrews, Pavia and Koln. Now, in 1451, it was to be the turn of Glasgow to rise to great heights in the new world of letters.

The son of an ancient Scottish family from Bedrule in the Borders, Turnbull was one of Scotland's great scholars and administrators. In his earlier life he had studied at St. Andrews, entered the Church, become Rector of Hawick and Canon of Lanark, and acted as emissary between the Pope, to whose Household he was attached, and James II. His ecclesiastical services had been rewarded by his elevation to the See of Glasgow, and his lay services with the offices of Keeper of the Privy Seal and the Great Chamberlainship of Scotland. Already a wealthy and powerful man, his decision to found a new university in Scotland was possibly an attempt to compete with the Bishop of St. Andrews and further enhance the importance of his own See relative to that of his rival. Possibly, however, his ambitions were more altruistic, and like many other medieval radicals, he could see a new way of life approaching in the light shed by the new learning.

As the older universities varied in age, so they varied in reputation and in organisation. Paris and Oxford were recognised as corporations of teachers (*universitas magistrorum*), Bologna as a corporation of scholars *(universitas scholarium)*. The Bull of Pope Nicholas V. specifically stated that the new institution at Glasgow was to enjoy the same organisation and privileges as his own university—Bologna. Theoretically, and to many subsequent generation of students ideally, this meant the introduction of a system of government by a *Dominicus Rector,* himself elected by the body of students; but in fact, another section of the Bull overcame the democratic element implied here, by appointing Turnbull and his successors in the See of Glasgow, to carry out the duties of Rector personally and without election.

The actual constitution of the University was drawn up by Turnbull. The rigid system of a *Universitas*

Magistrorum was to be slightly modified by the introduction of some of the more democratic elements present
in a *Universitas Scholarium;* the best features of the
systems of teaching followed in Koln and Louvain were
to be added to a basis of instruction modelled on that of
St. Andrews; Faculties of Art, Law, Theology and Medicine were to be established, adequately housed, and financed
from the revenues of the See.   This constitution, however, commendable as it was, never came into operation
in its entirety, for Turnbull died in 1454 and his successors failed to share his enthusiasm for the new project.

During the next hundred years, the only part of Turnbull's constitution which took root was the Faculty of
Arts, for it alone possessed the buildings and financial
endowments necessary to enable its survivial.   The
original buildings of the Faculty of Arts were probably
situated in the Rotten Row, but after 1460 a "College
of the Faculty" in High Street, was gifted by Lord
Hamilton.   In 1467 this property was extended by a
former student's gift of an adjoining tenement, and in the
next century endowments from Mary, Queen of Scots and
from the Town Council, further extended the buildings.
By this time (c.1550) the Master of the Faculty of Arts
had become *de facto* head of the University, and the
Rectorship and the Chancellorship had tended to decline
into ornamental appointments.

The University was little scathed by the Reformation
and from then onward gradually developed a sturdy
independence common to all the Scottish Universities, but
conspicuously absent abroad.   The main changes were
embodied in a *Nova Erectio* of 1577.   Here the word
Faculty ceased to mean Faculty of Arts, and came to
include only the masters of the College, or the occupants
of the newly created Chairs in Divinity, Medicine, Law,
Hebrew, Church History, Astronomy, and Anatomy. The

masters who taught Arts subjects were known as Regents, and the new constitution converted the post of Principal Regent into that of Principal of the University. The inspiring genius behind these changes, and also behind the ensuing re-establishment of Glasgow in the world of letters was Andrew Melville. Through his immense personal energy, Melville introduced an intellectual and material wealth which had hitherto been unknown to the University. When in 1580 he left for St. Andrews the University had been completely revitalised and had gained enormously in dignity and prestige.

Like the Reformation, the religious upheavals of the seventeenth century had little effect upon the University. Indeed, during this period sufficient funds were accumulated to enable a further expansion. Between 1635 and 1658 the main buildings of the beautiful new College of Glasgow were opened on the old High Street site. These buildings, of which several fine etchings survive, consisted of an inner and an outer court or quadrangle, and the range of buildings which separated the two courts was crowned by a tall graceful steeple. As had been the tradition from 1460, students continued to reside within the college, but eventually, in the early eighteenth century, all the accommodation came to be required for classroom purposes. During this period the governing body continued to be the Faculty, presided over by the Principal, though the Senate (a larger body which in addition to the Faculty included the Rector and some of the lesser teachers) and the Comitia (all the members of the University) still retained some degree of power. Except for a few brief lapses between 1690 and 1726 the students maintained their right to share in the election of the Rector, but the power thus conferred upon them was very slight.

In the course of the eighteenth century the University

grew enormously. The number of students increased from under four hundred to over a thousand, and new Chairs were created in many subjects, including Mathematics, Greek, Latin, Logic, Moral Philosophy, Natural Philosophy, and in various branches of Law, Medicine and Divinity. During this century James Watt carried out in the college classrooms his experiments on steam power, the Foulis brothers set up their University Press and brought fine printing to Glasgow for the first time, the Academy of Arts flourished and held regular exhibitions in the college buildings and quadrangles, and Adam Smith developed his economic theory for the *Wealth of Nations* while lecturing from the Chair of Moral Philosophy. In 1783 William Hunter, a distinguished anatomist and a graduate of Glasgow, bequeathed his magnificent collection of paintings, books, anatomical preparations, and zoological, geological, and archeological specimens to the University, and to house these the first Hunterian Museum was erected behind the college and opened in 1804. Bonds of mutual interest between the people of the town and the members of the University rapidly strengthened during this period, and by the beginning of the nineteenth century the new industrial Glasgow had become fairly proud of its seat of learning, and began to feel responsible, in a moral if not a financial sense, for its future welfare.

Politically, however, all was not well at the turn of the century within the University itself. The newly created Chairs in the important and growing subjects like Medicine, Engineering and Science, were treated with little respect by the holders of the older and established Chairs, and were entirely excluded from places on the governing body, the Faculty. This situation persisted well into the nineteenth century, discontent gradually mounting among both teachers and students, until at last, in 1826, a Royal Commissioin was appointed to inquire into the matter. Sensible proposals were put forward, but the advice was not taken until another thirty years of anachronistic government made a thorough revision of the 1577 constitution unavoidable. The Universities Act of 1858, supplemented by a further act of 1889, gave out the new constitution. The four Faculties originally envisaged by Turnbull, and two new Faculties, of Science and Engineering, were set up on a basis of mutual equality; the Senate absorbed the powers of the old Faculty; the University Court became responsible for finance and property; the General Council represented the interests of the graduates and the Students' Representative Council, originally an unofficial body set up by members of the Dialectic Society, was officially recognised as representing all the undergraduates of the University. Stimulated by this recognition, the students soon demonstrated a greater awareness of their corporate existence by founding in 1885 a Union, and by establishing four years later a newspaper of their own, the *Glasgow University Magazine*. Their political clubs also began a new lease of life, and now that the Rectorial elections had been freed from the interference of the Professors, they were the more hotly contested by the student societies. Women students were first admitted in 1892 when Queen Margaret College was incorporated into the University. Ten years later a Women's Union was founded, and when the buildings of the Queen Margaret College were taken over by the B.B.C., this was housed in the former Men's Union on University Avenue. Just before the Great War there were almost 3,000 students in the University, and since then the number has risen to over 7,200, of whom 1,400 are women.

Meanwhile the middle nineteenth century had seen a change of site for the University. By 1840 it had become obvious that the " Old College " was no longer large enough to house the greatly expanded departments, and industrial Glasgow was rapidly crowding in to impair the beauty of the fine old seventeenth century buildings. In 1864 the site in High Street, after negotiations lasting over a period of eighteen years, was sold for £100,000 to the City of Glasgow Union Railway Company. It had been occupied by the University for four hundred years, and it was not without grief that in 1870 a general migration was made to the new buildings at Gilmorehill. These had been erected from a combined fund subscribed by the University, the government, and the citizens of Glasgow. Two main portions of the seventeenth century college were re-erected—Pearce Lodge, formerly the Entrance Gateway, and the Lion Stairway, which had once led up to the Fore Common Hall and the Principal's House, and which now leads down from the front of the University to the Principal's Lodging. The " hurry-bell," which is rung for five minutes before lectures, and the panelling of the Senate and Court Rooms have also survived from the old site.

Since the transference was made, expansion has been so great that a whole range of new buildings has come into existence. Many of these belong to the scientific departments, but the Reading Room, opened in 1939, has since proved itself a boon to all students, and the Chapel, dedicated as a War Memorial in 1929, maintains the dignified connection of Church and University which has survived half a thousand years. A few hundred yards from the Chapel, the new atomic research pile leads us into the future.

THE GLASGOW UNDERGRADUATE

By JAMES BRIDIE.

> *James Bridie, Dr. O. H. Mavor, is to the University
> what Victoria was to the Victorians—he personifies
> a flavour and exemplifies a type. It might be thought
> that he will be remembered among us as the author
> of the " Anatomist," or the " Forrigan Reel," or a
> dozen other successful plays. Not at all. He is
> remembered as O.H., the G.U.M. cartoonist and
> G.U.M. editor, as the man who initiated our
> Saturnalia and invented our traditions. James Bridie
> is no mere playwright; he is and always will be The
> Glasgow Undergraduate.*

This is not an authoritative study. It is a haphazard
collection of personal impressions. It begins in 1904 and
fades out somewhere between the two Wars. At one time
I knew a thousand Glasgow undergraduates by name and
headmark. I now know less than a dozen. However
dogmatic I may become in the following pages, however
confidently I generalise, I hope that you will keep in mind
these limitations and that I am fully aware of them.

A friend of mine once said, "Students think that people
think them a lot of fine, dashing, devil-may-care fellows.
They are wrong. People think them a lot of ticks." One
interesting thing about this truth is the separation of

students from people and the lack of understanding that
exists between the two groups. People have always tended
to judge harshly any privileged class. Students are a
privileged class who have not yet reached the age and
experience that teach them to be conciliatory. They are
like the new Civil Service.

In 1904, at the age of sixteen, I stopped being a schoolboy and became a student. I was given a latchkey and a
small allowance. Out of the latter, I bought a bowler hat
and a pipe. I then began to consider deeply the nature of
this change that had come upon me.

I was still under the governance of teachers. I must call
them " Sir " and lift my hat to some of them (not all)
when I met them in the street. On the other hand, they
were not empowered to beat me. I was allowed to insult
and mock them by stamping, singing and shouting through
part of their lectures, and, at first, they seemed to have no
means of knowing whether or not I did any work and not
to mind much if I did not. The technique of avoiding
their attention was child's play to an ex-pupil of the
Glasgow Academy.

In the class room, the teacher did most of the talking.
I was seldom or never invited to rise in my place to have
my ignorance scarified. Attendances at these talks was
compulsory but unnecessary. Consequently I very early
lost the thread of the series. It is difficult enough to hold
the attention of a sixteen year old boy for a solid hour on
end, and it is more difficult when the missing of important
clues makes the subject matter more incomprehensible.
The lectures I attended quickly became to me intolerable
jargon, heard in circumstances of great discomfort. I
insulated myself as well as I could by writing nonsense
blank verse under the pretence of taking notes. Now and
again I paused to listen to a joke; but the jokes were not
often very good.

This kind of thing was not a novelty. In my schooldays I had learned to protect myself from madness by not listening to stuff I did not understand. I arrived at Gilmorehill virgin of any knowledge of Greek and Mathematics and survived unsullied by the elements of Chemistry and Physics.

There were, it is true, examinations. To meet this difficulty, the booksellers had prepared little catechisms designed to deceive the examiners into thinking that the examinee knew something about the subject. The stock answers could be learned by heart a day or two before the examination. My own trouble was that I was not what actors call a good study. Cribbing was another way, but I thought it unsporting and did not practise it. More than once a professor refused me a class ticket. Then real ingenuity was required and I never found mine wanting.

These are not personal impressions. This is autobiography. This will never do. Certainly, for all my boasting of a wide circle of acquaintance, I only knew one undergraduate really well. With characteristic bland impudence (really a mask for misgiving) he pushes himself between me and my page. It is right to say that, as he settled down seriously to the agreeable existence of a Glasgow Chronic, he began curiously to pervade the place. But he was not the only tick on the old bell wether. Nor were all his contemporaries such idle and cunning brutes.

The most exciting thing about the change from schoolboy to student was the new experience of being thrown into close contact with a huge variety of human beings. In my day the variety was even greater than it is now. So long as matriculation fees were paid, anybody could linger at the University for as long as he liked. We had drunkards in their fifties. We had foreigners of every shape and hue. We had rich men's sons and poor men's sons. We had fully developed madmen and embryo saints.

We had Runyonesque horse-players and gamblers, many of them veterans of the South African War. We had poets and peasants. We had even a scholar or two. We had Rabelaisians and prigs. We had dirty men and clean men. We had even some women students, who were known, in those days, as lady students, and very circumspect and lady-like they were. Or so I am told. The Union, in those days, was a club, not a dance hall.

The men, or " Gentlemen " as they were proud to be addressed, gave the College of Glasgow what character it possessed. The refining influence of Queen Margaret College was only dimly felt and, take us all over, we were monastic.

When I recall individuals, my sense of the richness of the place is intensified. There was a poet, who wore a cap, a morning coat and knickerbockers. He was reading divinity and physiology. He had had his intellects unbalanced by a near collision of two Clyde packets, on one of which he was purser. He had been sold to the Freemasons by Sir George Adam Smith for undefined purposes and used to write to the King, Mr. Asquith and the Principal about it. Some of his poetry was very good, some very bad. I learned from him how to converse with men of letters. He had the root of the matter in him.

There was a living legend called Roderick, who looked like some great prehistoric beast and carried his quota of alluvial soil. He was a divinity student who had come from St. Andrews. He was very strong and could propel a sixteen pound ball over forty feet. Indeed, when he was preaching at a Highland parish (these things could happen) he finished his stumbling reading of one of Principal Rainy's sermons by announcing that, although he might not well be able to expound the Gospels, he was the finest putterer of the weight and t'rowerer of the hammer in the whole of broad Scotland. It was he who told some embarrassed young girls in his congregation that they could giggle, giggle, giggle, but they would all go to Hell.

Another divinity student of those days, on his way to a student charge, took off all his clothes and threw them and his sermon out of a railway carriage window. Fortunately for him, a lady who pulled the communication cord pulled it opposite a place where X's cousin was a sergeant of police. Wrapped in a blanket, he sat in the police station and drank whisky, while a young policeman on a bicycle went back along the line for his clothes.

I could write a good deal about the divinity students of my time. It is strange to read in the papers that to-day's Fathers of the Church are accused of knowing nothing about life. I should have thought that some of them were not ill-informed.

I wonder what has become of James Aubrey Fair Boyd and of Zeek. Death has swallowed up many of the others. I cannot think that these two have drawn their pay packets. Aubrey came from California. He had lost one arm in an accident with a circular saw, but was otherwise extremely handsome. He wrote very good prose, but his leading characteristic was a child-like faith. If Satan had told him to cast himself from a precipice, he would have done so without question. And undoubtedly something or somebody would have borne him up.

One morning, when he woke up in strange, exotic surroundings and discovered that he was in a greenhouse . . . But this will never do.

W-ll--m C-nn-ngh-m, best of all Librarians, has the faculty of picking out specimens from his enormous acquaintance and (by his neat, informative and brief notes on them) giving the impression at once of individuality and of multitude. He has the same orderly mind as had the poet Milton, who gives us the impression in the work known as Paradise Lost that we know quite intimately all the devils in Hell. I have no skill in such synthesis. I go rambling on, telling stories, sometimes funny, sometimes not. At the hinder end there is none of the impression on my audience that I wished to convey. Nothing but exhaustion and confusion.

Mind you, I could give you not a bad picture either of Aubrey or Zeek. But neither of them is a typical student, and neither picture would help to give you the correct sense of unity in diversity. What is the use of telling you that Zeek was a lanky, peering man, the fifth in a generation of militant atheists, who could juggle with plates and once wrote of his heroine that her hair was the bright, Titian red of newly painted cart wheels? We were not all at all like that. One of us toured with a travelling Fair and took on all comers in a boxing booth with no knowledge of the Art of Self Defence, apart from half a dozen tricks that would have led to his expulsion by the Boxing Board. One of us ran away to sea and took part in a mutiny, before he was sixteen years old. Another passed all his examinations by tearing a textbook in two and carrying it into the Examination Hall in the pockets of his heavy overcoat. Yet another filled Lord Curzon of Kedlestone with confusion by the rapidity and impudence of his repartee. Another still, fought singlehanded the gallery of the Princess's pantomime before he was rescued by the police. One more made the Sheriff of ———shire tipsy.

Now look what I have done! I have given the impression of unbridled riot, of eccentricity and toughness, and undergraduate life was not, in my day or at any other time, any such thing. As T. S. Eliot would say, " That is not it at all." Not at all.

I have mislaid my alembic. I do not seem to be able to distil the essence of the Glasgow undergraduate.

I am as you have already gathered, playing for time

A celebrated billiards match in my day ended in a draw, no scoring. I have a lingering, subconscious hope for that happy issue as between my reader and me. But I must work up to some sort of coda.

In a study of the Glasgow Undergraduate, it is a positive disadvantage to know some of the answers at the end of the book. I see too many of my fellows from start to finish. This part of their lives is telescoped into what they became. I know that so and so and such and such died on the battlefield, became respectable, crashed ignominiously, ended in a mad house, ruled a colony, achieved a million pounds, a fellowship, a popular pulpit, a rich wife, a reputation, a peerage, a pig farm, five years penal servitude, a Secretaryship of State, a panel practice. Speculation in futures—all the delight of curiously regarding undergraduates—is spoiled. The beautiful question marks are ironed out into dull straight lines.

I think that the main characteristic of the Glasgow undergraduate (I do not know how it may be now) was that he quickly found his own feet and learned to stand on them. A Scottish University is not a Welfare State. I am told that a certain number of green ladies and inspectors has been appointed and charged with the duty of wiping the undergraduate's nose for him; but it is an elusive nose. Meredith said of Joe Chamberlain that he had an adventurous nose. So has the Glasgow undergraduate. The tapir or the elephant or even the Chancellor of the University has nothing on him. It is a questing, powerful, sensitive organ. It is a very valuable organ in the microcosm into which he finds himself precipitated.

In Glasgow, they do not put a ring through the student's nose. We have few traditions and almost no conventions —an extraordinary thing in an institution five hundred years old. I know what I am speaking about, because I invented most of the traditions myself. In the event, we do not turn out a very polished article, but the article is usually highly individual. Even when we send our scholars to one or other of the finishing schools in the South, they are not finished. The jagged, cutting edges are seldom smoothed off.

Glasgow College has never imposed a type on its alumni. Their only headmark is having no headmark Their manners are all sorts, from good to terrible. Their idiosyncracies are their own.

This resistance to environment perhaps puts the Glasgow student outside the common stream of culture. Indeed, he is often very ignorant of what is going on among the thinking portion of the population. It also makes him impossible to describe, to assess, to valuate, to classify. Thank God for that. I shall no more attempt it.

GLIMPSES OF SCIENCE

By ERIC REEVES.

In this article, Eric Reeves, a student in the Faculty of Science for four years, calls for a closer appreciation of the importance of Science in the University. He refers to some of the more notable features of the past, especially in the Natural Philosophy Dept.

It is a contemporary tragedy that no scientist is immune from the taunts of the "cultured " if he knows nothing of Spinoza or Scott or Sayers, and yet his persecutors can live quite freely, knowing nothing of Science or the scientific method. So it is that literateurs can fill the University Magazine month after month with their private laboratory work, while the scientists pin themselves faithfully to their microscopes, and talk shop in coffee room groups. Possibly 't is this invalid ostracism which has been partly responsible for the social conservatism of those who dabble with test tubes and photographic plates within the University. Yet in every academic institution to-day, the most vital and important work is that carried on in the Science departments. In a five hundred year old University there should surely be a little familiarity between those who decry and those who practise the Sciences.

When the subjects which now constitute Natural Science were first taught in the Old College, they were presented to students as part of a curriculum which constituted " Arts." The field of knowledge was restricted to the principles then being laid down afresh by the initiators of the new era of understanding. The instruction was given by the Regents, qualified in all four departments of learning, Greek, Logic, Ethics and Physics (which included Mathematics and Astronomy). To-day, the *training* of scientists is the primary task of men well-versed in the wide field of Science, but comparatively ignorant of the principles of Ethics or Greek. On the other hand, one no longer expects the Professor of Humanity to be familiar with the molecular structure of an alcohol.

Towards the end of the 17th century, the influence of the Renaissance had been felt to the extent that the ever-growing store of knowledge of West European civilisation necessitated a greater measure of specialisation, and in 1727 the need was so pressing that four professional chairs were established, one of which was Physics. The first occupant of this chair was Robert Dick, who, though no great scientist, demonstrated the investigations then being made in various parts, by initiating an evening class in Experimental Philosophy. Dr. David Murray records in his " Memories of the Old College," that in 1755, Professor Robert Dick, M.D., advertised that he " will begin a course of Philosophical Lectures and Experiments on Thursday, 23rd December, at 7 o'clock in the evening." The course included Mechanics, Hydrostatics, Pneumatics, Optics, Astronomy and " a methodical arrangement of Animals, Vegetables and Minerals." His students included a large number of the then-growing class of artisans in the town, as well as those students studying for M.A. Robert Dick was responsible for the association between James Watt and the University, when in 1756, he recommended that Watt should be appointed instrument maker to the University.

Upon Dick's death in 1757, John Anderson was appointed to the chair of Physics—at that time he was Professor of Oriental Languages. His relations with the University were anything but cordial, and after years of quarrelling, he eventually broke with the professional body and upon his death, directed that his estate should be used to establish a new University, to be called Anderson's University. Since he left only £1,500, his wish that there should be four Faculties and 36 professors could not be satisfied. The institution was designed primarily for the great number of artisans and small manufacturers and their sons, and ultimately became the Royal Technical College. This alone must be considered as an achievement of Anderson, even though it did come after his death, but apart from this, he made no contribution to Science. His opinion of his colleagues can be estimated from this extract from his will—" the professors in this University (Anderson's) shall not be permitted, as in some other colleges, to be Drones or Triflers, Drunkards, or negligent of their duty in any manner of way."

When John Anderson was plaguing the University authorities, two great scientists were working in the Chemistry Department and the Natural Philosophy Department of the old college—Joseph Black and James Watt. Black, still unmindful of the concept of heat as a form of energy, was investigating the manner in which a liquid cooled and boiled, and eventually arrived at the idea of latent heat. His work which led to the establishment of some of the microscopic attributes of heat, was of fundamental importance at that time. His versatility was paramount, for as well as occupying the position of Lecturer in Chemistry, he was Professor of Anatomy until 1766 when he moved to Edinburgh. James Watt had been introduced to the Newcomen steam engine by Dick, and he accomplished his early work on the steam engine in his room in the Natural Philosophy Department. Watt was also responsible for many of the larger installations in the College, including the old observatory on the Dowhill in 1754. The expenditure on Science at that time was hardly extravagant—£500 was spent on a new Chemistry laboratory, complete with new furnaces, the standard equipment at that time. This hardly compares with the cost of the apparatus of the Chemistry Department which twentieth century students know.

Lord Kelvin was by far the greatest scientist that Glasgow has ever produced. Son of the Professor of Mathematics, he graduated at 17 years of age, and at 22, was appointed to the chair of Natural Philosophy. William Thomson, as he then was, was at once a first class mathematician and an expert craftsman, although perhaps his greatest contribution to Science has been as an experimentalist. Here was no man content to repeat the established theories for the benefit of his sudents—Thomson *engaged* in Science; he produced theories, and took his classes with him along new paths of knowledge. He had no research staff other than his students, and the latter, for the first time in the history of the University, learned to use their hands as well as their heads, a very noble past-time. Thomson was recognised as the master of accurate measurement, and if the collection of his instruments in the present Natural Philosophy Department is inspected, his fine practical mind is at once recognised. William Thomson was one of the many great scientists of the new mercantile age, and his life spanned that great period of progress; it started when Faraday was conducting his experiments on electro-magnetism, and when Carnot and Joule were laying the foundations of thermodynamics, and Thomson's life was used to further the work of those men. His academic life ended when Sir J. J. Thomson discovered the electron, the particle which heralded the atomic age.

That is why Lord Kelvin left nobody behind him, when his energies failed—his work was accomplished and there was nothing else of fundamental importance to be done in that field.   Dr. David Murray was a pupil of Kelvin's and he describes him in these terms—" genius of the highest order coupled with sound judgment and practical ability, passionate earnestness and deep reverence; a modesty and simplicity of character, seldom met with."

Throughout the 18th and 19th centuries, new chairs in the scientific subjects were established.   A chair in Mathematics was founded soon after 1727—a chair in Medicine had been in existence since 1713, but it would require a separate article to deal with the history of Medicine in the University—Astronomy in 1760, Chemistry in 1817, Botany 1818, Civil Engineering in 1840.   These chairs were occupied by people great and small—Robert Simpson, the famous geometer, was a Professor of Mathematics at the time of Robert Dick.   Later still, of course, the Faculty of Science was established, and degrees in Science were awarded.

Notwithstanding the fact that the buildings which at present house most of the departments of Science were erected only 30 years or so ago, the infernal noise which for the past year has been coming from that quarter, heralds vast and important extensions.   The atom has been split, and the whole theory of Physics and Chemistry is in process of being constructed all over again.   Modern is posited beside Classical, and these buildings are being erected to further our command and understanding of that which is termed " modern."   The activity which will transform both departments into veritable beehives will form a dual process which has never been seen here before, on such a scale, namely the training of scientists and the discovery of new realms of understanding.   The biological sciences are not affected to the same degree, but in Physics and Chemistry, research workers are engaging in a world-wide task, the task which is common to every University which can afford a particle accelerator, or the intricate equipment of the crystallographer. The palmy days in which Kelvin revelled, when Science was a study necessary for the " cultured," have disappeared, to be replaced by an urgent, fluid, organised enquiry, striving to keep ahead of a world eager for rapid progress. In this enquiry the University of Glasgow will play its part.

For almost five hundred years Glasgow has given Scientists to the world. We can be confident, that the names of those she gives to the new world of Science, which in 1951, lies unexplored before us, will rank unashamedly with the names of the past.

QUEEN MARGARET STUDENTS' UNION

By STROMA DUNCAN

President of Queen Margaret Union.

It has been said that the phrases " an officer and a gentleman " and " a woman student " are both contradictions in terms. The Officer must defend himself, but the woman student has Queen Margaret Union to speak for her. Stroma Duncan, the President in the Fifth Centenary Year, describes the organism and the organisation which is Queen Margaret Union.

When the Duchess of Atholl officially opened Queen Margaret Students' Union on University Avenue, the nomadic existence of its members seemed to be at an end. Travelling from Buckingham Street by way of Ann Street and University Gardens, the Union was, in February, 1932, firmly established in the University grounds. As the building was originally intended to accommodate less than half its present number of members, which for the last few years has verged on the thousand mark, another change may eventually have to be made. This would be unfortunate, for it would be difficult to find a more suitable or more pleasantly appointed building in which to pursue the aims of the founders of Queen Margaret College Union, which was instituted on March 28th, 1890 " for the

promotion of social intercourse, to keep former students
in touch with their successors and with the college, and
generally to promote the interests of the College."

The College itself was founded in 1883 by a group of
men and women, led by Mrs. Campbell of Tullichewan
and Miss Janet A. Galloway who was Secretary of the
College until her death in 1909. From that date until her
retiral in 1935, the head of the College was the Mistress,
Miss Francis H. Melville, now Dr. Melville and Honorary
President of the present Queen Margaret Union.

Until 1935, when their classes were transferred from the
College in Queen Margaret Drive to the University buildings in Gilmorehill, women were matriculated students
both of the College and the University and, by the request
of the women students of that year, the official title
"Queen Margaret Students" maintains the link between
the present women undergraduates and the generation
which founded Queen Margaret Hall, Queen Margaret
Settlement (now the University Settlement) and Queen
Margaret Union.

The stress which the original members of the Union
placed on " social intercourse " showed that they were
fully aware of the wide significance of the University
Education for Women for which they were appealing.

The fact that the University on whose door they were
beating was non-residential made that recognition infinitely
more valuable.

The founders of Queeen Margaret College realised
that the right of admission to classes, for which they were
appealing, was only a part of what was entailed in
membership of a University, and by the formation of a
club for University women they provided the medium
through which the new phenomena, the woman student,
could derive the fullest benefit from, and make her
contribution to the community which she was entering.

The Queen Margaret Student inherits not only the traditions of the University, common to all undergraduates but also the attitude of mind of her predecessors and their recognition that although in the academic sphere, the emphasis is, of necessity on the student, it is in her own Union that the " Woman Student " finds scope for the development of both the qualities implicit in her title.

When the men evacuated the Union on University Avenue, it was adapted to the needs of women students. The changes which were made, together with these features and customs which were accepted in their entirety, form a commentary, in however slight a form, on the new occupants.

The business of undergraduate life is still transacted in the same rooms and in a similar fashion. The management of the Union is in the hands of a Board of twenty-four members of which twelve, including the President, Secretary and Assistant Secretary are matriculated students. Of the other twelve members, nine, including the General Adviser to Women Students, are members of the General Council of Queen Margaret Union and are elected by the Council to serve on the Board of Management for three years. There are also three graduate members, one of whom must be a graduate in Law. The student and graduate members of the Board of Management are elected annually by Union members. Of the six sub-committees, the Executive, House and Treasurer's Committees are concerned with the more strenuous business of Union Management, but the Debates, Entertainments and Library Committees under the guidance of their Conveners have an equally important task, and provide the more obvious attractions of Union activity.

The old Debating Hall, the present Common Room is still the scene of Debates, Dances, Lunchtime Meetings

QUEEN MARGARET UNION

Photo by Fenton Studios

and Concerts. The Debates are usually run on Parliamentary lines with the President and Convener of Debates of Queen Margaret Union acting as Speaker and Deputy-Speaker. Except in the case of a Private Members Debate, bills, drawn up by the political clubs are submitted before they are debated, to the Debates Committee, composed of the Executive, the Q.M. Presidents of Political Clubs, the Q.M. President of the Dialectic Society and two co-opted members. A record of the proceedings is compiled and later published together with advice and criticism, by the Clerk of the House and her two Deputy Clerks. Prizes for the best Maiden Speeches are awarded at the end of each Debate and a Shield is presented at the Annual General Meeting of the Union to the Political Club whose members have contributed most to the standard of Debates during the year.

Debates, Club Meetings and discussion. The traditions common to any student community, remain the same.

The changes are more subtle, but the authentic atmosphere of a woman's club, which the founders of Queen Margaret College Union meant to create is undeniable, and if the gulf between the woman and the student seems to find its practical illustration in the Coffee Room roof which separates the cubicles, a wonderful relief when the dance ends at one and the last tram leaves at twelve, from the study on the other side, any Q.M. member can show you the corridor which joins them. The corridor between the cubicles and the study is as easy to find as the link between the woman and the student, if you know the Union.

When the woman undergraduate acknowledges the implications, and earns the title of " woman student " she justifies the belief which the founders of Queen Margaret College had in their Union. They might have been surprised at the extent to which women, thanks to their efforts, are participating for the first time in the centenary celebrations of the foundation of the University, but they would undoubtedly have acknowledged that in her own Union and through its activities the woman student finds the opportunity to make her unique contribution to the University community.

THE RECTOR AND THE UNIVERSITY

By COMPTON MACKENZIE, O.B.E., LL.D.

Compton Mackenzie, the author and philhellene, was Rector of the University of Glasgow from 1931 *to* 1934. *His election was a new departure in the history of that office. In this article he describes the function of the Rectors through the life of the University.*

THE first Rector of the University of Glasgow was David Cadyow, the sub-dean and precentor of the Church of Glasgow, and although the Pope's bull of foundation gave to Bishop Turnbull and his episcopal successors as Chancellors the same authority over doctors, masters and scholars as the Rectors exercised in the *studium* of Bologna the Chancellors in practice delegated this authority to the Rectors and added to it further jurisdiction.

The Rector, who was elected annually at a general congregation upon the Feast of St. Crispin (October 25th), was in effect the ruler of the University. He incorporated new members ; he summoned and presided over general congregations of the supposts. It was his duty to read the University statutes in public once a year in order to prevent the supposts from pleading ignorance of them, and he had to ensure that all the acts and resolutions of the University during his term of office were set on record. The Rector was also the judge in all cases that affected members of the University, deriving as as he did from the Bishop civil and criminal as well as academic jurisdiction. To guard him against mistakes in the exercise of his judicial functions he was enjoined to take advice from his four deputies as men skilled in law. The Rector appointed the bedellus and the notarius ; he could nominate one of the senior beneficed masters to act as Vice-Rector in his absence. His costume on ceremonial occasions was to be stately ; a white staff was to be carried before him and on the greater feasts a silver rod was to be substituted for the white staff. At the annual election the supposts met at the house of the outgoing Rector, escorted him to the meeting place, and when the new Rector was elected escorted him back to his house. Indeed, the Rector was always being escorted either to the Cathedral and back for some service or to University functions, and in 1490, possibly at the Rector's own suggestion, the statute requiring him to go to Church on Sundays in procession was repealed.

The first Rectors were usually canons of Glasgow, but members of the nobility who held benefices were frequent. In 1513, that black year for Scotland, Patrick Graham, a brother of the Earl of Montrose, was elected Rector six weeks after Flodden; in 1514 his re-election was contested, the first time we hear of a contested rectorial. Graham defeated James Stewart, a Canon of Glasgow, and was re-elected in 1515 and 1516.

The four deputies of the Rector were not intended to represent but to advise him ; they were not appointed by the Rector nor by the Nations, but were elected like the Rector by the four intrants, who themselves were elected by the Nations. It is to be noted that the intrants then elected two and even three of themselves as deputies; and they usually took a hand in the Rector's appointment of the bedellus. It was after the Reformation that the Principal began to emerge as an important officer of the University. His was a Crown appointment, but he was not allowed to absent himself for any length of time from the University without the permission of the Rector, the Dean of Faculty and the Regents of the Arts; if he spent three nights outside the College without leave, Crown or no Crown, the appointment was annulled.

Towards the end of the sixteenth century the election of the Rector was fixed each year for the month of March. The electors, still divided into Nations, now included students as well as masters, and for nearly a century from 1593 onwards the Rector chosen was almost always a minister of Glasgow or near by. Upon his election the Rector usually nominated the Principal, the Dean of Faculty, and several masters and regents as his assessors to whom were frequently added one or two ministers from the city and surrounding country. This was a development of the deputies of pre-Reformation days and might be considered a kind of embryo of the University Court of nearly three centuries hence.

As late as 1670 the University was still claiming to exercise jurisdiction outside the law courts, a remarkable survival of benefit of clergy. In August of that year a student called Robert Barton was tried before the Rector, Sir William Fleming of Ferme, and four Assessors, on the charge of having shot and killed Janet Wright, servant to Patrick Wilson. The Procurator-Fiscal for the University and Andrew Wright, the nearest of kin to the dead woman, preferred the indictment and a jury of fifteen were empanelled. The prosecution could not produce satisfactory witnesses, but before the jury gave their verdict they asked to be secured from detriment in case they were afterwards challenged for taking part in a trial of the University's right to hold which they were not clear.

The Rector and his Assessors duly guaranteed the jury against detriment, whereupon they found a verdict of not guilty. One asks how the University would have handled the problem of hanging that student if he had been found guilty. Perhaps the jury were worried too and thought the easiest way out of possible trouble was to let the prisoner go.

During his office as Principal, William Dunlop, being a devoted Orangeman, managed to disfranchise the students in the Rectorial Election on the grounds that in the unsettled state of affairs after Dutch William's accession the convening of the students for such an election might lead to disturbances. The students appear to have lost their votes without a struggle. However, when Principal Dunlop was succeeded by Principal Stirling in 1701 the quarrels between him and the masters led the latter to promote an agitation among the students for the restoration of these votes. For some years a compromise ruled. The Principal and the Professors having chosen the Rector, assembled the students, announced their choice and expressed their hope that the students would agree with it.

Sir John Maxwell of Pollok, a friend of Stirling's who was Rector from 1691 until 1716, the longest term of office on record, supported the Principal in his pseudo-elections; but in 1717 seven of the Professors joined with the students to elect a Mr. Muir as Rector according to the ancient and unrepealed statutes. Principal Stirling and his supporters appealed to the Duke of Montrose, the Chancellor,, and a Royal Commission was appointed to enquire into the divisions and disorders in the University.

The war went on for ten years until at last in 1727 a Commission of Visitation laid down a body of statutes by which the University continued to be regulated until the passing of the Universities Act of 1858.

The Commissioners ordained that the Rector was to be elected annually on November 15th by the " matriculated members, moderators or masters, and students in the said University." The electors were to vote by Nations, in the ancient manner, each Nation choosing a procurator and an intrant to collect the votes and declare the result; if the votes were equal the outgoing Rector was to have the casting vote. The boundaries of the Nations were reaffirmed, but Clydesdalia was changed to Glottiana, Thevidalia to Loudoniana, and Albania to Transforthiana.

In 1761 quarrels broke out again and went on for nearly forty years. The main controversary was over the provinces and powers of the Senate and the Faculty, but finance was also a sore point. The Senate, formerly the University Meeting, consisted of the Principal and Professors, the Rector and the Dean of Faculty; the Faculty excluded the Rector and paradoxically the Dean of Faculty. The Principal was Chairman of the Faculty; the Rector was Chairman of the Senate but was empowered to nominate another member of the Senate as Vice-Rector, who presided in the Rector's absence and sometimes unconstitutionally exercised the Rector's powers, now mostly financial, as a Visitor.

The Faculty numbered fourteen members, the Senate sixteen. The Rector's Meeting had managed to control most of the administrative side, but in 1771 and 1772 decisions by the Court of Sessions put most of the administrative powers in the hands of the Faculty.

In 1813 two of the Professors proposed that application should be made to Parliament for an Act to confer upon the Senate the power of electing the Rector. Nothing further was done, but when Kirkman Finlay, a former Member of Parliament for Glasgow, was chosen as Rector

D

in 1819 the students put up a candidate of their own to contest the election of 1820 when in the ordinary course of events Finlay would have been re-elected. This candidate was Francis Jeffrey, who to the chagrin of the Professors was elected. The hostility of the students to Finlay was due to their suspecting him of being privy to the Senate's plot to disfranchise them.

Before this election Rectors had contented themselves with a few words of thanks at their installation; Jeffrey introduced the long address on some topic of interest to the students. He devoted much of his oratory to restoring good feeling between the professors and the students.

In 1822 the vote of the Nations was divided between Sir Walter Scott and Sir James Mackintosh, the latter having a large majority of votes in the total poll. Jeffrey gave his casting vote for Mackintosh who after holding office for two years was now called on himself for a casting vote. In that 1824 election Glottiana and Loudoniana voted for Lord Brougham; Rothseiana and Transforthiana voted for Sir Walter; for the first time there was a third candidate— Henry Mackenzie, the Man of Feeling, who received only a few votes. Mackintosh tried to get out of giving a casting vote, but the Senate pressed upon him his duty to obey the Statutes and finally six months later in April 1835 he gave his casting vote for Brougham.

There were three candidates again in 1826 when Thomas Campbell was elected by the votes of three Nations and a total of 280 votes; Sir Thomas Brisbane received 189 and Canning 83. Campbell was unanimously re-elected in 1827 and in 1828 he was proposed for a third year. Although in earlier days Rectors had been re-elected many years in succession, for a long time now custom had decreed two years as the tenure of office. Campbell's opponent was Walter Scott and two Nations voted for each poet. Thereupon Gavin Gibb, having been appointed Vice-Rector by

Campbell the year before, gave his casting vote for Scott, who was declared to be elected. A protest was immediately lodged against the Vice-Rector's casting vote as not conforming with the statutes. Scott in the circumstances declined to accept office, and a meeting of the *comitia,* that is the whole membership of the University, ordained a fresh election. Campbell arrived from London to encourage his supporters and after protests and counter-protests three Nations voted for the poet; Loudoniana voted for Sir Michael Shaw Stewart who had replaced Scott as a candidate.

The Principal and several of the Professors conducted a campaign against Campbell's election for the third time, declaring that it was invalid because he had no residence in Scotland. However, after a long battle Campbell was admitted to office and his rectorial address won over many of those who had opposed him. In this he promised the students " assembled not at his bidding but by their own spontaneous enthusiasm, that he could never refuse them any proof of the power of his interest in their welfare." Although opposed and obstructed by the Principal for the rest of his term of office Campbell devoted himself practically to University affairs. Among other things he urged upon the Universities Commission the advantage of the students continuing to elect the Rector.

The Commissioners in 1830 recommended the Constitution of a new body to be called the University Court and to consist of seven members—the Principal; the Dean of Faculties; the Minister of Glasgow; an assessor nominated by the Chancellor; an assessor elected by the Principal, the professors and the graduates; and the Rector. The University Court was to review all regulations of the Senate and to be a Court of Appeal in every case; it was also to control the finances of the University. However, the University Court did not come into existence for nearly another thirty years when it was created by the Act of 1858.

The last Rector in the nineteenth century to play an active part in the life of the University was Henry Cockburn who was elected in 1831, re-elected the following year, and in 1833 tied in the Nations with Professor Sir Daniel Sandford but had a majority of individual votes. The Vice-Rector when called on to give a casting vote declined, so Cockburn as the outgoing Rector had to do so and voted for himself because in his view Sandford as a professor in the College was ineligible.

Gradually, as the years went on, the Rector of the University receded further and further from University life, and his election which by the Act of 1858 was reserved for the votes of the students became merely an opportunity to honour some prominent man of the day, almost always a politician. It was clear that the Act of 1858 intended the Rector to represent the interests of the students in the University, but, so long as the students were content with a figurehead for their own often transitory political opinions, it was idle to expect a Cabinet Minister to spend any of his busy time on Rectorial duties which had become no more than a dim memory.

Then in 1928 Cunninghame Graham was put forward as the candidate of the Glasgow University Nationalists and nearly succeeded in defeating the Prime Minister. Three years later the writer of the present article was elected exactly one hundred years after Henry Cockburn's first election. Looking back twenty years, he can now see that his success may have been due less to his nationalist politics than the pledge he gave his supporters that he would take as active a part as a contemporary Rector is able to take in the life of the University. Since that 1931 Rectorial election at Glasgow the students of Aberdeen and Edinburgh have followed the example set by Glasgow (St. Andrew's had already given up the habit of choosing political candidates for their Rectorial) and to-day it can be affirmed that the students elect their Rector in the expectation that he will do his duty as such. It is not an arduous task, for no official duties are left to a modern Rector except the chairmanship of the University Court if he choose to occupy that chair. The old quarrels between the Rector and the Principal have long been forgotten. The Rector is no longer called upon to perform the invidious duty of impugning some professor for spending too much on his house. The Rector is no longer involved in acrimonious assertions of privileges usurped by the Senate. Perhaps, if the Professors and the students fell out, the Rector would again be called upon to present the case of the students and if both sides lacked common sense a disagreeable state of affairs might be precipitated. However, it is difficult to imagine a dispute in these days provoking any kind of crisis between the University authorities and the student body. In any case the Students' Representative Council, which began as a voluntary association in 1886 and was given statutory recognition under the Act of 1889, would more probably be the protagonist rather than the Rector.

Nevertheless, the Rector of a Scottish University to-day has a duty of precept and example outside the field of studies, and if he leave nothing behind him except a tradition of good manners and consideration for other people he will not have failed in his duty towards his young constituents.

TOWN, GOWN AND STUDENTS

By Charles C. Robson, M.A.

The author of this article was born in Arabia, the son of a Professor of Arabic. He served in India and Burma during the war, being mentioned in despatches. On demobilisation he matriculated in the Medical Faculty and has since taken an active part in the corporate life of the University.

For more than forty years, there has been no major disturbance between the students of Glasgow and either the Town or the Gown. This must be almost a record, because, although the Scot is by tradition an industrious student, he has never been loth to challenge authority whenever cause should arise and sometimes even when the cause could not be immediately apparent to an impartial observer. This is probably just as true to-day as ever it was, but with changing times, methods have changed. Rioting is no longer regarded as an expression of youthful high spirits, and any student who set upon his professor with sword or quarter-staff or their modern equivalent might expect to be rather severely treated. To-day, authority does not take too kindly a view of exuberance, so protest must be made in a more decorous, constitutional manner. There was a time when things were different.

In the beginning, the students were drawn mainly from the sons of the Scottish nobility and these were often high-spirited young men with no great desire for learning. They found Glasgow an extremely congenial place in which to sow their wild oats, the taverns and ale-houses being as numerous then as they are now and less under the influence of the Magistracy. In the early years students were required to live in the College or in its immediate neighbourhood, but on occasion, possibly when they felt the pressure of work too great, some of them would take up residence in town and indulge in such pleasures as were to be had. During Andrew Melville's tenure of office, a son of Lord Herries fancied he had a grievance against the authorities. He had a considerable following among the riff-raff of Glasgow, and so, collecting a band of them, he sallied forth and encountered the procession of masters and students. One of his friends brandished a sword in Melville's face and used threatening language, but Melville continued on his way, even restraining the students who were about to join battle on his behalf. When Lord Herries heard of his son's escapade, he immediately came to Glasgow and ordered him to apologise to Melville on bended knee.

Not all fathers were as strong in their support of authority. Some years later, a student called Boyd, took exception to being rebuked in public by his regent, John Melville. Having unsuccessfully attempted to " frame " Melville on a charge of using undue physical violence, Boyd took up residence in town. A few days later, in company with a friend named Alexander Cunningham, he attacked Melville as he was passing through the High Churchyard with two friends. Cunningham was armed with a sword and Boyd with a truncheon, but when Melville resisted strongly, Boyd took to his heels and Cunningham was disarmed. The Rector, together with the

Provost and Magistrates ordered Cunningham to appear at the scene of his crime bare-footed and bare-headed and there crave Melville's forgiveness. This he refused to do, declaring that he would burn the College and slay the masters. The matter was taken to the Privy Council who ordered Cunningham to obey the decree on an appointed day under penalty, if he failed to do so, of being imprisoned or being declared a rebel. On that day, the full academic procession made its way to the High Church-yard, where Cunningham appeared dressed in fine clothes and supported by his father, the Earl of Glencairn, with four or five hundred friends and followers. Cunningham announced that he was willing to obey the decree if any one would dare to take his submission. Melville, unmoved by this show of force, replied that he was ready, where-upon Cunningham submitted meekly in the prescribed manner. His friends had not been told why they had been summoned to Glasgow and thought the whole performance an excellent joke. After spending a few days celebrating in Glasgow, they returned home.

In these two cases, only individual students were involved with the authorities, but in the years following the restoration of the Stuarts in 1660, there was continuous and sometimes violent unrest among the body of students as a whole. It was at this time that students of Glasgow were described as being frequently "tumultuating." As might be expected, they supported the cause of the Covenanters and after the battle of Bothwell Bridge, many wore the blue ribbon of the Covenant. As the University upheld the established authority of the country, many students were brought before the Court to answer for their conduct, and punishments were made more severe. The most serious was expulsion or " extrusion and exter-minating out of the University in the most opprobrious manner," and a series of fines was laid varying with the rank and birth of the offender. These measures did not prove very effective. One student, when being examined, addressed the Archbishop of Glasgow as " Sir " and not as " My Lord." When asked whether he knew whom he was addressing, he replied that he did and refused to yield the principles which he held.

One year a force of Highlanders, mainly from Athole, was brought down into Ayrshire to force the landowners to promise that they and their tenants would have no dealings with the " intercommunicated ministers and vagrant preachers " who were holding their services in remote parts of the countryside. The Highlanders were none too particular in their methods and took every opportunity of looting the homes of the country folk. They were more successful in this than in the main object of their journey, and on their return carried a miscellaneous collection of pots and pans, bedclothing, wearing apparel and other articles. At the bridge over the Clyde at Glasgow, two thousand of them were opposed by a body of students with a number of young men from the town, who informed the Highlanders that they would not be permitted to cross until they had given up their booty. This they eventually did, but it is not related how the students managed to carry out this rather astonishing feat of arms.

On another occasion the students were less successful in a battle with some " Highlanders." There was a space of ground round the observatory called the High Green which was barred to students. One day, much to their astonishment, they saw some men of the Highland Light Infantry disporting themselves on the Green. Summoning their forces, they scaled the walls and attacked the soldiers. At first they had some success, but reinforcements arrived from the nearby barracks and soon the students were being very roughly handled. Fortunately some officers appeared on the scene and the infantry were called off before too many heads were broken.

In the defence of the rights and privileges of the University both students and masters were united in a common cause, though their methods were different. The University claimed the right of jurisdiction over the students for acts committed both inside and outside the University and this right was confirmed by successive kings and Acts of Parliament. In 1670 the University even tried a student who was charged with the murder of a servant. There was considerable doubt whether the University had the authority to hold a trial on a capital charge, and the jury demanded security against action being taken against themselves if the proceedings should be declared illegal. After hearing the evidence, they declared the student not guilty, but if he had been found guilty, the University would have been faced with the problem of carrying out the sentence, which, in all probability would have been death by hanging.

As the years went by the Town Council became more and more dissatisfied with the position and began to challenge the University's authority. Both students and masters resisted this encroachment on the University's privileges, each in their own way. When a Bailie imposed fines on a number of students, the University demanded that he return the money, and threatened that if he did not do so, legal action would be taken, the costs of which would require to be borne by him. Some years previously more vigorous action had been taken by the students when a number of their comrades had been clapped in jail. They seized the keys of the prison, stormed the jailor's house and set the prisoners free. This angered the citizens of Glasgow who marched on the University with drawn sword, entered the inner quadrangle and fired a number of shots into the unarmed students. On only one other occasion did the people of Glasgow become sufficiently roused to attack the University grounds. At the beginning of the last century, considerable difficulty was found in obtaining sufficient bodies for the teaching of anatomy, only the bodies of criminals being permitted to be used for dissection. The medical students, taking the law into their own hands, began resurrecting bodies from the graveyards. This, incidentally, was before the time of Burke and Hare. Once again a mob attacked the students, but this does not seem to have dissuaded them to any great extent, because twenty years later the North Quarter Friendly Churchyard Guard Association was formed to police the graveyards and prevent the removal of bodies from the graves.

With the passing of successive Local Government Acts, the University gradually lost its right to try students for acts committed outside the University or to claim students arrested by the police, but many other rights and privileges were retained. The University precincts have always been considered outwith the province of the police and only on a few occasions have members of the force set foot in the University in a professional capacity. One winter's day in 1865, a rather hectic snowfight was in progress in the College grounds. A crowd gathered outside and began to join in. Lord Kelvin, who was passing by, feared that the situation might get out of hand and asked the police to disperse the crowd. Instead, they arrested a student. He was rescued by a rush of students, but another was promptly arrested. As tempers were bcoming frayed, Lord Kelvin led the police with their prisoner through his laboratory and out a back door. Meanwhile, police reinforcements had arrived, but instead of dispersing the crowd and preventing further trouble, they stationed themselves along the railings of the College. The temptation proved too great for the students who found the police an easy target for their snowballs. Exasperated beyond control, the lieutenant in charge of the police ordered his men to climb the railings, but the barrage of snowballs proved too much for them. Finding a gate a short distance along the railings, the police entered, drew their batons and charged the students, driving them into the inner quadrangle. After a rather strenuous battle, the police were withdrawn, taking with them four students, but leaving two of their number behind. These were speedily ejected by the medical students who kept their coats, hats and batons as trophies. While the scrimmage was in progress a detective had been chalking the backs of a number of students, and when the students began leaving the College, four more were arrested. In all, ten students were arrested and later released on bail.

On the following day they were brought to trial. The case against four of them was found not proven and two were fined ten pounds each. The case against the four who had been arrested later was dropped, as the police learned that a student had noticed their detective chalking the backs of the students and had chalked the same mark on the backs of a number of innocent bystanders, making the police mark useless for identification. The Glasgow Herald had been very strong in its condemnation of the students and had published a rather inaccurate account of what had happened, so when the sentences were announced, a party marched to the Herald offices and ceremoniously burned copies of the paper. A collection was made to defray the expenses of the fines and the twenty pounds were changed into coppers. When they were presented at the police office, the lieutenant at first refused to accept the coppers on the grounds that they were not legal tender, but eventually entered into the spirit of the joke and accepted payment.

Since the " flitting " from the High Street to Gilmorehill, only two incidents have occurred which rival those of the past, and these are mentioned elsewhere. Nowadays, among the students at any rate, there is no longer the feeling that they are a body separate and distinct from the Town. Probably the most potent factor bringing about this change is that by far the great majority have their homes in Glasgow. Possibly Charities Week acts as a sufficient outlet for their surplus energy.

Once again there is talk of a " Covenant " and once again the Anatomy Department is in difficulties, but amongst those present, there are no signs or portents that past conflicts and rivalries will be resurrected.

A G.U.M. SIDELIGHT

From material provided by
ARCHIBALD DUNCAN THOMSON.

*Archibald Duncan Thomson was not unknown to
readers of G.U.M. in the 1900's and has taken a keen
interest in the magazine ever since. Possibly no living
person knows more about its early years than he does
and in these pages he describes the birth pangs and
adolescent illnesses of the early Glasgow University
Magazine.*

On the 11th of January, 1873, the " Acadamie " an
Aberdeen University weekly states, " we have just had
brought to our notice the first number of the Glasgow
University Magazine and, although somewhat hurt by
finding therein utter ignorance of our own being, we
nevertheless welcome heartily the birth of this brother,
who being seemingly a monthly is naturally bigger and
better."

But surely this cannot have been G.U.M., which was
wholly unborn at that time? Ah yes, here we have the
truth : " On Tuesday, 5th February, 1889, and every
working Tuesday after that till 26th March, at Marr
Grieve's in Jamaica Street, under S.R.C. auspices." That
is the real birth notice.

Of course, it was by no means an easy birth. The 1880's
saw a great deal of stirring amongst Scottish studentdom.

Each College sprouted first an S.R.C., and then each S.R.C., although scarcely weaned, sought a printed mouthpiece. First, the Aberdeen "Alma Mater " in 1883 ; then the Edinburgh " Student " in 1887; finally, St. Andrews with its " News Sheet," later to become " College Echoes." This places Glasgow well-nigh last.

The S.R.C. at Glasgow certainly discussed the idea of a journal at pretty well every meeting—ordinary and extra-ordinary—from 1885 onwards. And in 1887, Alex. Ralston, journalist-to-be, tried to inaugurate a Scottish University Review—a dream that was finally scotched by Robert Horne (Editor of G.U.M., Volume 5), when he declared that each University already had its work cut out to look after its own magazine.

Then an evening paper offered to open its columns to articles on specific subjects, such as University Reform ; but first it called for the head of a certain Brother Pelican who was running a weekly called " Gilmorehill Jottings." So successful was this Pelican that he refused to give up, and four years later G.U.M. was shrieking loud and long at the " Disobedient Councillor," begging him to " act the Judas no longer " and not to sell his soul for 30 pieces of silver. This latter was actually ten shillings a week, quite a useful sum in those days. Not for yet another four years was identity discovered, and by that time the " bird " had flown.

But to return to the birth of G.U.M. In January, 1888, S.R.C. Secretary, Harley by name, was instructed to seek costs of printing from Aird & Coghill and from Lyons for a " Weekly, Fortnightly, Monthly of 8, 12, 16 pages, with a circulation of 2,000." This figure represented a copy for every matriculated student—rather a tall order.

And so, the following December, a magazine was recommended. It was laid down as 12 pages Weekly of awkward foolscap size, to cost one penny, and containing

College news, society news, reports, poetry, and various contributions on music, drama, and literary articles. It was to be run by a committee selected by S.R.C.—two members from each faculty—and it was to choose its own chairman with a deliberative and a casting vote. Chairmen there must have been, but none of very great weight, worth or width, and this is the last we hear of them. Even the minute of the special meeting to vote on all this in January, 1889, has been torn out of the book!

But what of the £.s.d. side of things, without which nothing much can be done in this world? Well, one outlay at least was spared them, for in 1886 the Senate had granted S.R.C. a glass-covered notice-board, and Mr. Harley had a locked letter-box. However, this letter-box caused so much trouble—the key as often as not missing—that in 1892 G.U.M. was presented with one of its own. This original G.U.M. box, incidentally, was stolen one dark night during an "election" raid.

The life-blood of the magazine—advertisements—was just as badly needed in those early days as it is now. Just over two pages were eventually gathered in. One page at 2 guineas went to the Students' Book Emporium (our old friend Stenhouse), another page was shared by Forsyth, White and Hilliard, and a quarter page was taken up by Lizars. The " Micawbers " in charge reckoned on selling 1,500 copies an issue, but even so there was a good risk of loss. So, S.R.C. was persuaded to put up a £10 guarantee and then, but not until then, the order was given for " full steam ahead."

Of the first issue, 1,500 copies and then a further 500 went before sundown on the first day. The second issue went almost as fast. But thereafter sales dropped steadily to an average of 1,100 copies per issue, leaving a loss on the year of £3 17s. 6½d.

The second volume, under a new management except

for Harley, got off to a late start owing to lack of material —a lack that has hampered G.U.M. ever since. It contained the same sort of reports and long articles, but in addition it ran a gossip column called " Don't Tell," a forerunner of the famous "Fleeting Hour." It ended the year 7s. 1d. in pocket after repaying a £5 12s. 5½d. guarantee loan. Volume Three saw a change of printers, to Thomlinson's of Partick, who kept it until Hay Nisbet took over with Volume Ten. The third volume was a considerable success " literally," thanks to the work of Madge Wildfire (William Parker Hanks) with his poems and cartoons. The 1,187 average sale and the 14s. loss on each issue raised awful fears, the final loss being over £6. But 30s. of this was the disowned debt of the —— Society (just use your imagination).

Volume Four was of a reduced format, but its price was 2d., including a nice pink cover. This volume had the first recorded chief editor, John White. Its budget did little more than balance. The next volume reverted to the 1d. price and netted £9 10s. under the editorship of Robert Horne, whom the Tories later made Chancellor of the Exchequer!

The next year, under Stokes Little, who started the pernicious habit of resigning at Christmas, there occurred a catastrophe that well nigh ended the G.U.M.—the Advertising Agent defaulted with £75. An action was authorised, and £25 was retrieved, which with G.U.M.'s own £17 reduced the deficit to only £33! There followed a debate as to which—if any—of the Handbook or G.U.M. was to continue, a debate that was won by G.U.M. But for the next session, all costs had to be reduced to a minimum, no new blocks or photos, and so on. But from that volume forward, G.U.M. ran its own advertising! And it was student acumen as well as student writing that made G.U.M. what it is to-day.

E

MINUTE BY MINUTE IN THE LIFE OF THE STUDENTS' REPRESENTATIVE COUNCIL
By DONALD MACMILLAN.
PRESIDENT OF S.R.C.

Donald Macmillan has done more than any other student to make Council a dominant force in the University. He has served as Secretary for three years and is a former Editor of the Handbook. In the year of the Fifth Centenary he is not only President of S.R.C. but also Convener of the Fifth Centenary Committee. For a great many years Mr. Macmillan's hobby has been studying Medicine, a hobby which was interrupted by seven years' service with the H.L.I.

" All the world's a stage,
And all the men and women merely players;
They have their exits and their entrances;
And one man in his time plays many parts."
SHAKESPEARE.

How well this fits the life of an undergraduate, for our life here is brief—or should be—but a minute in the time of our University, and often when we leave there is little evidence that we were even there. But always there are those few who leave something of themselves, something which through time, assuming an air of respectability, ultimately graduates to a tradition ; and so beside the orthodox, age-old " Meal Monday," there springs up that *enfant terrible* " Daft Friday." Curiosity about the origins of these events sent me to G.U.M. and the minutes of S.R.C. where I found little, for they came into being without thought and such spontaneity leaves no record. There was revealed however, another facet of student life. It was fascinating to watch Council's beginnings, to see it stretch forth like an unsteady child ; to approve of its growth and its vitality but sometimes to sigh at its folly.

Although it was not till 1889 that the Universities (Scotland) Act officially sanctioned an S.R.C. at Glasgow, the students held a General Meeting at the end of 1885 to consider a constitution, similar to that already existing at St. Andrews. The first recorded minutes, those of the 6th of February, 1886, were concerned with the setting up of a Union and concluded with a vote of thanks to the anonymous donor for his generous gift of £5,000 for that purpose. At that meeting, too, the representation of S.R.C. was discussed and a month later this was put into rapid effect ; as now, each Faculty had its representatives and, in addition, Council welcomed delegates from certain Clubs and Societies, who were invited to put forward claims for admission to S.R.C. (It is interesting to note that on the 20th March 1886, the Glasgow Foreign Mission Students Union was not admitted to Council, whereas the Total Abstinence Society was.)

Plans for the Union went steadily ahead until 1888, when it was necessary for Council to call a General Meeting of Students to arraign the Union for dereliction of duty :

"This meeting regrets the absence of the usual report from the Union Committee, strongly condemns the inactivity of certain members of that Committee and strongly censures the Convener . . . and the late Secretary . . . for culpable neglect of duty."

Because, or in spite of this meeting the Union got under way, though critics were always ready to prod or rouse its office-bearers. For instance the provision of meals, at that time, was incurring a steady loss and on 23rd March 1889 the question of a licence to recoup on the deficit was hotly debated, appropriately enough in the Biblical Criticism Classroom—S.R.C.'s meeting place.

" This meeting of the Students' Representative Council, specially summoned to consider the question of the Students' Dinners, expresses the opinion that the introduction of a licence would be detrimental to the best interests of the students and requests the Senate to take this protest."

This was carried by 29 votes to 2.

Shortly to be invested with powers contained in the Act of Parliament, the interests of Council now broadened considerably and, conscious of its duty to the Students, Council petitioned in favour of the Glasgow and Suburban Subway Scheme which was then before the Upper House. A member was appointed to give evidence before the Select Committee of the House of Lords, but unfortunately it is not recorded, whether or not he was called upon. Contact, however, was forcibly made with authority on rather a different level. It appears that the Senate, in 1889, committed the unpardonable sin of keeping a Graduation secret. So on 23rd November we read :

1.—" That this Council protest against the attempt of the Senate to hold the recent Graduation Ceremony in private and that without giving any notice of their intention to do so."

2.—" That this Council deeply regrets the outbreak of violence, the destruction of property and the attacks on certain of the Professors."

Motion 1 was carried unanimously, but the Secretary

(stout fellow) moved that the words in Motion 2 relating to the attacks on Professors be withdrawn. This was accepted but it was felt necessary to refer it to a General Meeting of students, which was convened with amazing rapidity one hour later, and there by 125 votes to 117 the Student body decided not to apologise for the attacks on members of the Professoriat. The enthusiastic meeting then went on to discuss a newspaper report (*Glasgow Evening News*) that certain of the sons of Professors had been responsible for the recent disturbances, but discretion being the better part of valour, the matter was dropped.

About this time the representative of the Conservative Club was Robert S. Horne, who in 1893 became President of Council, and, with his student indiscretions behind him was later to become Viscount Horne of Hillhead. For the next five years things were comparatively quiet ; Council moved from the Conveyancing Class Room to Biblical Criticism and back again . . .

There is a break in the Minutes from 1894-1905. A thorough search of Pearce Lodge, The Union and The Library failed to produce any sign and, as Secretary, I tried to trace the book through the columns of *The Times, The Daily Telegraph, The Glasgow Herald* and *The Scotsman*. The Secretary in 1909, Robert Gibson, M.A., B.Sc., had undertaken the same quest and his reply to my letter is worth recording.

SCOTTISH LAND COURT.

1 Grosvenor Crescent,
Edinburgh, 12.
27th June, 1949.

Dear Mr. Macmillan,

I have read with interest your letter in to-day's *Scotsman* regarding the volume of the Council Minutes for years 1894 to 1905.

Just over 40 years ago—1909-10—I was Secretary of

G.U.S.R.C. Like you I was distressed at the absence of these Minutes, for the remainder were full of interest and the Executive Minutes were complete.

I enquired of my immediate predecessor, James A. Hendry, later the distinguished and popular Professor of Midwifery at Glasgow, but he knew nothing of the missing volume. Neither did his predecesor, the Rev. R. E. Lee, nor did J. B. Galbraith. I managed to get the address of Robert Helier Napier who graduated in Divinity and had gone as a missionary to Livingstonia. I wrote him and had a charming letter in reply in which he described how, in his time, a predecessor of his had what he described in his letter as a " young fire " in his (the friend's) lodgings. In that way the Minute Book came to a sad and irretrievable end.

Napier's letter I backed up and added to the official letters I received during my secretaryship. That bundle, neatly tied up and identified by a sheet giving the dates covered by the letters, I left in the depositories of the S.R.C. when I demitted office.

It is unfortunate that you have not traced Bob Napier's letter. Had I thought it would go astray I would have made a formal report of the correspondence to the Council and duly entered the fact in the Minute Book.

Yours sincerely,

ROBERT GIBSON.
(Lord Gibson).

The Executive Minutes show that Council had much to contend with as the 19th Century drew to a close :

" January 24th 1901. Complaints being made that letters, sent to the Clerk of Senate received not even a formal reply, the Secretary was instructed to write him a private letter asking him for an explanation."

PEARCE LODGE

Photo by Fenton Studios

Women, everywhere attacking the realms hitherto sacred to men, had been admitted to the University. There were wild schemes to keep the two sexes apart. Indeed Heath Robinson could scarcely have imagined a more ludicrous contraption than that mooted for the Humanity Classroom. A partition was suggested dividing the room in two so that only Professor Ramsay could see the "monstrous regiment of women." This was carried further when at the Rectorial Installation of Lord Asquith, in 1907, the women were relegated to the back of St. Andrew's Halls, on the instructions of the Acting Principal who, however, came in for much public criticism for

" deliberately, on his own initiative, altering the arrangements made for the conduct of the Rectorial Installation."

Later, however, Council revoked its championship of the weaker sex and in 1908, after a prolonged discussion

" during which the financial, academic, and social aspects of the question were discussed, Council voted that the number of women students entering the University be limited."

The Senate was petitioned, at the same time, to ban the Queen Margaret Suffragette Society (now extinct).

Oratory flourished during this period 1909-1911, as a vigorous dialectic exercise rather than as serious debate. Those responsible included Robert Gibson, now Lord Gibson ; Osborne Mavor, Vice-President of S.R.C in 1909. then using the pseudonym " The Squid " rather than the now better known " James Bridie " ; Walter Elliot, " hands in his pocket, every brace button showing " ; John Boyd, now a member of Senate, and W. D. Robieson of *The Glasgow Herald* as the Chapel Convener. Elliot was censured by Mavor and cleared himself. Mavor was censured by Elliot and cleared himself. The heights to which oratory ascended are not recorded but the happy combination produced " Daft Friday." Earlier Council had the famous Johnny Mowat as Vice-President, and his contretemps with Lord Curzon, the Rector, was the talk of Glasgow. The Rector had been awkward in arrangements regarding the date of his visit but he finally agreed to attend on 24th February 1911. Before the Installation Curzon, with a certain amount of condescension, preferred his Address to the Executive Committee.

" I suppose," said the great man, " that lulls in my speech will be filled in with applause and whistles." Mowat, who had been irritably pacing up and down outside the group, flashed back " You had better see there are no lulls in your speech." " Ah," replied Curzon, " perhaps Mr. Mowat would be good enough to read my speech and approve of it." " Haven't time — studying for exams.—give it to him to read," thumbing in the direction of the harassed Secretary of S.R.C.

The Installation was attended by enthusiastic scenes and a Torchlight Procession was duly held . . . the inevitable happened. Council met at a later date to discuss the damages.

The first account of £9 19s. 0d. from Messrs. Henderson for repairs to the carriage occupied by Lord Curzon was debated. Mr. Graham moved and Mr. White seconded that Council do not pay for the account. The motion was carried. The account was sent to the Court for their consideration.

The second account of £18 18s. 0d. from the Manager of St. Andrew's Halls was submitted, and, after discussion, the motion accepting responsibility was put. Mr. Barr put a contrary motion that Council repudiate the account. Mr. Barr's motion was carried.

The Procession Convener moved that Council pay for the damage to two gas lamps (at Charing Cross) valued at £3 14s. 1d. This was agreed on.

It is interesting to note that the Treasurer, who was instructed to pay this account was the first man to be appointed to this position (1912), a post which Mr. George F. Todd, C.A., has held with distinction to the present day.

After the dynamic force of Mavor and Elliot left, inevitably it fell away—no Council could sustain such a pace. During the 1914-18 War it met but infrequently and held no elections, since the Principal ruled :—

" That S.R.C. came under the provisions of the Defence of the Realm Act and no elections should be held."

It started vigorously enough after the War with renewed attacks on Women Students. On 12th January 1919 Council discussed their attendance in Clinique at the Western Infirmary and voted that women be not admitted, the proposer in his argument stating that

" Mixed clinics were detrimental to men students, who stand back, on account of their innate politeness."

A year later, however, both sexes, side by side, were petitioning for better conditions in Clinique at the Royal Infirmary.

The Councils of the four Universities had been meeting since 1888 and had done much good work. The University authorities took a keen interest in their deliberations and often took part in some of the discussions.. In 1920, Edinburgh S.R.C. put forward the suggestion that Matriculation be increased and that the increase be devoted to the funds of the Athletic Clubs; Now 10/6 of every Matriculation Fee goes to G.U.A.C. Council also took an active part in the affairs of the time and Mr. Tudor Jones, now a Professor at Manchester, was the delegate to the Strasbourg Peace Conference, in 1919. From then until 1925 S.R.C.'s main activities were directed towards curriculum reform and in this had some success. On 4th March 1925 the draft consitution of the National

Union of Scottish Students was drawn up to replace the Inter-Varsities S.R.C. Annual Conference and this was the fore-runner of the Scottish Union of Students as it is known to-day.

Graduation at this time had again become more enthusiatsic and Council was forced to take a strong line. So on 11th February, 1926 :—

> " Council deprecates the inappropriate noise, pointless interruptions and absence of wit shown by a section of the students during Graduation Ceremonies ; and also the vulgar type of ragging indulged in after the ceremony, especially the removing of boots and the blackening of faces."

The proposer had just graduated in Arts !

In 1930 Council found itself in more trouble through entertaining some of Mr. Cochran's " Young Ladies " who had helped in the production of College Pudding. There were many charges of bribery and maladministration and a Committee formed by the " Good Government League " investigated the complaints.

> " On considering the charges we have found that many of them were based on such scanty evidence, that the Council cannot reasonably be asked to take any cognisance of them, and we deplore the rash statements which were put forward."

Council at this time took its full share in the work of the Inter-Varsities S.R.C.'s which had replaced N.U.S.S. The Freshman's Camp was instituted ; evening cruises were organised ; Charities Day was the responsibility of S.R.C. and the " Gilmorehill Globe " made an appearance lasting for three years.

The 30's also saw Stanley Baldwin as Rector, then Compton Mackenzie who was followed by that great gentleman Sir Iain Colquhoun. Now however, with war clouds threatening, the Oxford Group sprang into prominence with its plea for peace and, quick to reply, Glasgow Students, in the remarkable election of 1938 returned " Dick " Sheppard, Canon of St. Paul's, rejecting their own McNeile Dixon, J. B. S. Haldane and Winston Spencer Churchill. His triumph however was short, for the victor died within 8 hours of his election and the next election, held a year later, saw as Rector Sir Archibald Sinclair, who held office for the war years.

Once more returned from the wars and gamely facing the task of reconstruction the S.R.C again takes up its duties. Now permanently installed in Pearce Lodge, the oldest building in the University, it has been quick to respond to the needs of the time, so much so, that a permanent Clerk of the Council is now a necessity. The Minutes show the diversity of the work—Book Sales, Employments, Ex-Service Grants, I.S.S. and at present a share in the organisation of the Fifth Centenary Celebrations. Now as then, all this is only possible because there are those who feel the call of tradition strongly enough to give to the University as well as to receive from it.

THE LEGACY OF FIVE HUNDRED YEARS
By LORD BOYD ORR OF BRECHIN, D.S.O., M.C., LL.D.,
F.R.S.

> *Lord Boyd Orr of Brechin is one of Glasgow's most illustrious graduates. In a long association with the Scottish Universities he has been student, Professor, Member of Parliament for the Scottish Universities, Rector of Glasgow, and he is now our Chancellor. From 1946-47 he was Director General of the United Nations Food and Agricultural Organisation and for many years he has been an acknowledged authority on the international problems of nutrition and malnutrition.*

FOR five hundred years the University of Glasgow has been making its contribution to the growth of knowledge and to the education of men who applied the new knowledge to the evolution of human society. It should be part of the education of students and indeed of all members of " the congregation of the University " to get some understanding of the history of their Alma Mater and the legacy they have inherited.

On the annual Commemoration Day the Vice Chancellor preceded by the mace, itself nearly five hundred years old, ascends the rostrum and recalls to our memory those who by their benefactions made possible the expansion of the work of the University. It is fitting that we should

remember " our fathers who begat us." It is even more
fitting that we pay tribute to the many famous men of
science and learning, who, though not benefactors in the
material sense, contributed by their researches and studies
to the great advance in physical well-being and culture of
the past five hundred years and made the name of the
University famous throughout the world. Students should
leave the University with more than a degree which
qualifies them to begin their education in the profession or
walk of life which they have chosen. They should leave
feeling that their names have been added to the long list
of the Congregation among whom are men of the past who
shaped the present and that it is incumbent on them so far
as in them lies, to be the men of the present who will shape
the future. It is worth considering whether before each
graduation the professors in the various subjects or the
Deans of the Faculties might give a special lecture to the
graduands on the contribution made to their special branch
of knowledge by past teachers and graduates. In every
Faculty there have been some whose names are known and
honoured in all countries by those engaged in the study of
the subjects in which these men of Glasgow were pre-
eminent.

And when we remember with pride and gratitude the
work of these men as individuals we should also remember
what the University did as a whole especially in the early
days though the names of most of the " congregation " are
forgotten. In medieval times when this University was
founded there was a reverence for tradition, custom and
religious dogma which maintained the structure of society
as it had for long existed. But the time had come for a
forward movement. That movement came from the medieval Universities. At that time they gave vocational
training for service in church or state as they now do for
these and many other spheres. But the training was not

given in cloisters as in the dark ages. It was given in a new intellectual atmosphere. In the course of the training there was the exercise of reason with original thought and the inevitable discussion among men living together in a centre of learning. In the contact of theologians and philosophers with the enquiring mind of youth there arose freedom of thought and a new dignity of the human mind which blossomed in the Renaissance from which originated the age of reason and our age of science. That is the great legacy of this and other European Universities to the modern world.

The development of the atmosphere of enquiry and discussion was facilitated by the freedom of travel of European teachers and students many of whom taught or studied in more than one country. This brought about an exchange of ideas between men of different countries. With the expansion of this University under the energetic Principal Andrew Melville in the 16th century many foreign students came to Glasgow, for, as it was said "There is no place in Europe comparable with Glasgow for a plentiful and good cheap market of all kinds of languages, arts and sciences." Thus early did the University establish its reputation as an international centre of study.

This freedom of thought and free communication of men of science and culture is the great legacy of this and other Universities established five hundred or more years ago. It is more important for the promotion of human welfare than further technical advances letting loose new physical forces which human society is not mature enough to use wisely.

In our day an attempt has been made by a totalitarian state to suppress freedom of thought and expression and prostitute science and learning to political ends. In the present conflict of ideologies there may be a danger even in democratic countries that governments with increasing centralisation of power may think it necessary to suppress by rougher or gentler means those who hold views conflicting with the policy of the state. Freedom of thought and expression is the very lifeblood of Universities which must be above all politics. Any state which curtails that freedom condemns itself to arrested cultural and spiritual growth.

For five hundred years students and teachers with widely different inherited traditions and beliefs have met and mingled in the halls of this University. In their mutual intercourse and free discussion, in an attempt to get near to the eternal and unchangeable truth, the spirit of youth has developed and matured. From the gates of this and other Scottish Universities there have gone forth men who have had an influence on world affairs out of all proportion to the size of the population of this small country. We can look back on the past with pride and look forward to the future with courage and hope that on the thousandth centenary our successors will be able to give us the credit for handing on to them, enlarged and enhanced, the legacy we received from our predecessors.

ALMA MATER

By MAKHAN DUBE

> *The Auld Alliance between Scotland and France made it necessary that Scotland as a country should welcome the strangers within her gates. The Scottish Universities have extended that welcome to all who wish to study. Here is a West Indian student to tell how it feels to be fostered by a Scottish Alma Mater.*

It is difficult to withdraw from the tedium of undergraduate life, to view the passing months with calm detachment, and to find its true significance in the story of life. It is even more difficult to remain in the maze of student's activity and predict with any degree of certainty, which feature one shall treasure most and which least. The glamour and glory which now envelops certain days and events may dissolve, leaving them bare and pale. Colour and content may be imparted to what now appears colourless and insignificant. It is a trick of passing time— to distort and mock, to illuminate and glorify capriciously. With this awareness, I hesitate to write.

To be an undergraduate in a foreign country provides experiences which one does not always find delightful. This is particularly so when one studies in a country where the people have preconceived ideas about one's abilities and behaviour which one would like to dispel. Everything seems a double burden, with a double purpose, carried at disadvantages which again are multiplied.

But there are compensations which now appear negligible but which time shall magnify. It is impossible for the foreign student in Britain to-day to remain unaware of many features of British life. No amount of reading can teach him as much as he learns in a short period of residence here. It is true that he cannot pursue all channels of investigation which have caught his curiousity. But he cannot isolate himself. Some local problems affect him directly; most affect him indirectly. Nor can he resist comparing and contrasting the social system here with his own. It is a fascinating and valuable exercise. Indeed, he questions the value of everything new and strange. Much of this experience grows upon him. He is unconscious of it, but it remains in him ready to assert itself as occasion demands. His experiences here form a background which modifies his way of thinking forever.

These experiences are not part of the University curriculum nor of student life. A tourist or immigrant may learn as much. Nevertheless, it is true that every foreign student in Britain gains this extra-knowledge for which he is very thankful.

A West Indian student is especially pleased to study at Glasgow University. Of all the cities of Britain, Glasgow lies closest to his heart. The pages of West Indian history sing praises of thankfulness to this city and old University which was founded forty-two years before the discovery of our islands. From the very early days, the Clyde has played an important part in their development. It is difficult to imagine how much the West Indies owe to Glasgow and its University. The success of many crops, particularly sugar-cane, was due in no small measure to the fortitude of the plantation owners, amongst whom were many Scots. These men laid the foundation of an industry which is now the pivot of West Indian economy. This industry would have passed away long ago, had it

F

not been for the advances made in engineering and ship-building in this city. The sugar factories that dot the West Indian landscape, that form the backbone of the social as well as economic life, that hum noisily day and night at harvest time,—all bear the stamp of Glasgow's ingenuity and workmanship. The names, "Blairs'" or "Mirlees Watson" are probably the first words that a West Indian child may decipher for himself, as he gazes at an old wheel on a factory estate. Refining of raw cane-sugar was once a profitable industry on the Clyde.

Not only to the Faculty of Engineering, but to that of Arts also, are the thanks of the West Indies directed. Many Colonial Officers with the best qualities of the proverbial Scotsman, were trained in this Faculty. Energy, courage and that indispensible touch of human under-standing have characterised the successful pioneers from this school. The Scottish missionaries are to be praised also. For, in spite of pressure from every quarter, and strong temptation, they have remained true to their purpose of building schools and raising the standard of education in the islands.

It is not surprising therefore, to find that continuing this close association, this University has viewed with great favour and delight the establishment of a University College in the West Indies. It is the culmination of efforts in which the Universities of Scotland played a most glorious part. Its staff already consists of some members from Glasgow University and it is to be hoped that there shall be an increased intensity of an old and fruitful association in education.

Every West Indian student is mindful of his gratitude to the University and the city. This is a pleasant thought which cheers him on the cold and rainy evenings. He is cheered too, by names like "Plantation Quay" and

" Jamaica Street " which remind him of an historical and friendly link, just as the Scottish names of West Indian families shall remind him of Glasgow and the Clyde. When he finds himself in loneliness, and surrounded by dangers of every kind in a land of sometimes hostile hosts, he thinks of these things, smiles and takes heart once more. Long may this association grow, strengthened by personal friendships, sincere and new.

It is unnecessary for me to outline the facilities afforded by the University for academic studies.—Some students would say they are more than adequate—This is but a relatively minor advantage. As books become more available, and up-to-date reference libraries are established throughout the world, the foreigner grows aware of this. He may even feel cheated by being asked to attend the University to read books which he could buy more comfortably and learn more easily in his own land. Of greater value to him, therefore, are the hours spent in practical classes and demonstrations when he makes acquaintance with the techniques and equipment. Even greater is the influence of the personalities of the staff. He looks for the fire of enthusiasm which shall liberate new energy in him to satiate his pricking curiosity. For this he is grateful.

Great joy awaits the stranger on the day of his matriculation. Not only does he feel secure in being one of the large family of undergraduates, but feels not too unimportant when criers of the various student's bodies besiege him for his support. Their presence reminds him, perhaps for the first time, that some vigour and initiative amongst students has escaped the heavy hand of class-ticket labour and degree-hunting.

These bodies mean a great deal to all of us. For some, they are to be avoided. For a few they are ladders to local fame. For most, they are an essential part of University education. They constitute a feature which distinguishes the University from the high-school. They are the foundations of the much haloed, much despised, most hackneyed " corporate life."

It must not be thought that a student who is not a member of any of these clubs is not taking part in the advantage of corporate life or vice versa. The Men's Union and Q.M. Union, like Unions of other Universities, are much used meetings places. Here is ample opportunity for meeting the youths of the West of Scotland who come from many walks of life.

Often one hears complaints of the inadequacy of facilities in the University for social intercourse. But in most cases, the authors of these mutterings are either lazy or snobbish and advance them as excuses for their short-comings.

Perhaps, the limiting factor in the corporate life is the attitude of the students. Those who are friendly find ample opportunity to share a discussion or a jest. Those who are unfriendly, and are too busy with their self-importance, cannot.

The foreign student in Glasgow, although admiring the profusion of societies and clubs, is asked to make a difficult choice. In every case, he is asked to accept this and reject that. Most of the clubs which ask his support are religious or political. Both in religion and politics, hard-and-fast dogmatism faces him. A decision is to be made at a time when he feels himself on the threshold of knowledge, more inclined to explore freely than to accept and reject slavishly—Every small body seems to limit his range of activity, a path trodden innumerable times, in a West of Scotland fashion.

The only body which seems to open out into horizons unlimited and unexplored, which gives a touch of universality, and takes him out of his provincialism is the

Student International Club. This club—which celebrates its Silver Jubilee this year, has been almost a home to overseas students, and in it the clash of East and West, of North and South and of the other discordant forces makes it an invaluable testing ground for ideas old and new. Its membership recalls that of medieval universities, and its debates are no less polemic.

The Student International Club affords invaluable chances for members of all nations to learn of one another. One comes more closely to world and national problems there, than any amount of reading or lecturing could take one. It stimulates and makes one aware of a world much wider than one knew before. At its conferences some of the most able thinkers of the society speak freely on subjects of topical interest. It is part of University life which no student—at least foreign—would like to miss.

Notes on facilities for discussion would not be complete without mention of class-rooms and laboratories. None can deny that great friendships can be made between classes and even in them, particularly in practical classes. The stranger values this opportunity immensely, although he is often unable to appreciate a jest centred around a local character cartoon or group of phrases. The more quickly he is introduced to them, the sooner will he be able to enjoy the company, and even contribute to it.

Practical classes which are not too rushed are ideal for discussion. Perhaps the ones in Anatomy are the most full of argument—often not on Anatomical detail. The tempo of debate, the shattering contributions from intruding neighbours, the welcome interjection of " medical " jokes, the rapidity with which we go off at tangents, and the lightning return to anatomy when circumstances force us, make these classes some of the most restless and enjoyable in my University career.

The question of residence at Glasgow University is a

troubled one for the foreigner, and there is no system which makes his troubles any less. The University Halls of Residence are too small to make any real contribution, and he is left at the mercy of the often unscrupulous land-ladies, who are well-acquainted with the details of their profession. He is often a beginner in this mode of living.

The problem of residence has greater discomfort for colonial students here. As in other cities of Britain, doors are closed to him for reasons which are not disclosed truthfully and over which he has no control. One may maintain that the problem teaches him a great deal, but it would probably leave him less bitter if his wanderings were more comfortable, though no less revealing.

The Residential Halls, though small, fulfil much of the function which the University has lost in the increase of undergraduate membership. There is no better way to learn of the character of a people than by living with them. In these halls, there is fortunately a number of nationalities and in this respect they resemble the medieval Universities. They are almost colleges of the University. The opportunity for community life, for the esprit de corps, for arguments heated and frank, for making friend-ships strong and sincere, will always call gratitude from strangers far from their homes.

Any system which takes away the international spirit from these halls by refusing admission to, or making them unattractive to any nationality, does great disservice to them, and to undergraduate life. One would like to see these halls expanded to the size of the largest—but no further—and increased in numbers, maintaining through-out a new emphasis on their international nature. The stranger should take away from them memories, dear and sweet.

In the sphere of sport, there are golden chances of making friends and learning of them. For some, the sport sections form nuclei around which they drag their friends to entertainment of their own kind. To most, they afford hours of relaxation, of exercise, occasional glory and comradeship. It is a pity that more cups and trophies are not donated to more sections both in the University and amongst the Scottish Universities. Competition will raise the standard of performance not to mention the increased interest and enjoyment by all.

The vacational employment of students is of special interest to the student from overseas. It is often a necessity, financially and psychologically. The three or six months of vacation finds him spending at his usual rate or perhaps greater. He is often bored beyond imagination, and left to think how happy he might have been at home. The solution is work. It occupies his mind. It saves his pocket money and more. Furthermore, it gives him access to meet people, who are not undergraduates, and find how human they are. None of these considerations are made by the Employments department of the S.R.C.—which does very good work—and these students are left to boredom in which to brood hostility and revenge. To desire to invite a stranger to his home is a trait which readily distinguishes the English undergraduate from the Scottish.

After a rapid review of some aspects of undergraduate life it is now left to say quite frankly what benefits are looked upon with greatest gratitude. The colonial student arrives here with a vision of Britain which is shattered too soon for his peace of mind. The luxurious dwelling-houses of colonial officers, often surrounded by lawns, and their haughty arrogance impress the colonial child from his earliest years. The education system, so largely dominated by Ox-bridge, builds up his picture of Britain—a glorified large-scale Stratford on Avon. The names in English history and science ring in his ears—glory upon glory.

Perhaps history does glorify, but what his eyes see and

his ears hear are even more significant. He wonders whether these days of glory are gone foreve⸱. There may be some aspects of contemporary life in Britain which may read well in history books, but what strike him most are the things which are unsung and of which he had never heard nor read. They have suddenly broken into his consciousness.

After the initial shock, a period of instability ensues. In this period there is great questioning and research for new values. This is a most exciting stage, full of danger, and challenge. He must find his own way.—no longer in " Stratford on Avon," but very much down to earth.

New value appears in the unsung, which formed the framework of his now discoloured picture; the hard-working labourers in the fields, on the seas, in the mines. The millions of men and women who fill the small essential roles in any organised society are unsung in the pages of history. But they carry on, giving painful birth to genius, to immortalise their trials and errors, ambitions and successes, despair and happiness. It is in these simple folk that he finds not only the latest of his admiration, but soon shares with them " their tenderness, joys and cares." This transformation, perhaps permanent, which gives him a new love for the human being, seems the greatest benefit, and most unlimited joy.

It might appear that I have been hostile in my remarks on my University. It is only out of my interest in her that I have appeared to be so. After all, I consider some of my best years spent under her guiding arms, and would like to see others share the greater opportunities as under-graduates.

These years shall remain most memorable in my life. The academic studies shall serve me well, but greater still, the experience I have gained in my friendships here. I thank the members of the University and the citizens of Glasgow for taking me and other colonials in as one of their own. They may rest assured that wherever on this globe I may be, the name of Glasgow and its University shall find a most tender spot in my heart, till the end of my days.

THE UNIVERSITY AND ART
By T. J. HONEYMAN

*Dr. T. J. Honeyman graduated in Medicine from
the University in 1916. After serving in India and
Salonica with the R.A.M.C. he was for some time an
assistant in the Physiology department before going
into general practice. Later he was on the staff of
the Royal Infirmary and assistant to the Professor of
Medicine. In 1929 he forsook Medicine and became
a fine art dealer. He has been director of the Lefevre
gallery and since 1939 he has been director of
Glasgow Art Galleries. In 1943 he was awarded the
St. Mungo Prize for his services to the city.*

IT is probably emphasising the obvious to remind ourselves
that the history of art is as often illustrated by the diaries,
memoirs and biographies of the period as it is by the art
productions.

The historians have told us that Puritanism, in its
extreme forms, changed the religious and social life of
Britain. The banishment of beauty led quite logically to
the destruction of pictures and statues, etc., since, it was
argued, these things are dangerous and therefore they
had better be destroyed. It is difficult to say when the
reaction actually set in. In painting, it began with the
importation of artists from the Continent. Patronage
was given very grudgingly and it was quite a long time

before anything worthy to be defined as a " National School " came into being.

The Glasgow Town Council records show that in July 1626 the Provost and Bailies made an agreement with one, James Sanderis, " to instruct the bairnes within the borough in music." Later, in 1708 and 1712, one or other of the Scougalls was commissioned to paint portraits of King William III and Queen Mary II and Queen Anne.

About this time, Francis Hutcheson matriculated at Glasgow University (1711). After a period in Ireland he returned to the University, having been elected Professor of Moral Philosophy in December 1729 by a majority of one vote. Adam Smith, who attended his class in 1740 spoke of him as " The Never-to-be-forgotten Hutcheson." Whether he has been remembered sufficiently is debatable. The claim of his biographer, Professor W. R. Scott, that Hutcheson undoubtedly wrote the first modern treatise on aesthetics, has in recent years been amply supported by a revival of interest among modern writers on the subject, especially in America.

While there is no evidence that Hutcheson had any real appreciation for the work of the great Renaissance masters, or that he even saw them, there now seems to be no doubt that he played a prominent part in awakening the country to the value of art in everyday life. In his book, *An Enquiry into the Original of our Ideas of Beauty and Virtue,* under the heading " Of the Power of Custom, Education and Example as to our Internal Senses," he says this :

" *Education* and *Custom* may influence our *internal senses* where they are antecedently, by enlarging the Capacity of our Minds to retain and compare the Parts of complex Compositions : And then if the finest Objects are presented to us, we grow conscious of a Pleasure far superior to what common Performances excite. But all this presupposes our *sense of beauty* to *be natural*."

In his day, as in ours, there are always the Philistines who refuse to let the aesthetician get away with this kind of philosophical approach to the appreciation of beauty. For example, Sterne in 1799 wrote this :

" Hutcheson in his philosophic treatise on beauty, harmony and order, plus's and minus's you to heaven or hell by algebraic equations—so that none but an expert mathematician can ever be able to settle his account with St. Peter—and perhaps St. Matthew who had been an officer in the customs, must be called in to audit them."

It is customary when speaking or thinking of the University's link with the plastic arts to start with the Foulis Academy and Andrew and Robert Foulis, the brothers who created it. The probability is that Hutcheson is the real source because, apart altogether from his place in the history of ideas, it is more than certain that his influence and encouragement of the two brothers led eventually to the idea of an Academy of Art. The whole purpose of Hutcheson's teaching and his own personal example are reflected in the aims which inspired Robert Foulis to set out on his great enterprise :

"Whoever imagines that he has anything to offer for the good of his country ought to expose it freely to examination, since the great law of goodness is, to do all the good in our power; and if upon examination it is found chimerical, the worst is a little ridicule; and to be able to stand this, rather than suppress what may possibly be useful is the part of a good man. If there is genius what a pity it should be buried, if methods can be found of giving it light, by introducing Establishment proper for the instruction in the beautiful arts, placing before generous youth the most excellent models,

inflaming their minds with a nobler vision of equalling them."

Too much should not be made of the fact that the Foulis Academy antedated the Royal Academy by some 15 years. They were both private enterprises and each of them had its detractors. In the case of the Foulis Academy, Robert records : " There seemed to be a pretty general emulation who should run it down most." But the University gave the venture much encouragement, assigning to it the lower part of the new library for a place in which to teach the scholars. And, although the attempts to obtain public assistance to help to meet the very large outlays were not very successful, two Glasgow merchants, Archibald Ingram and John Glassford (names perpetuated in two important civic thoroughfares) were among his supporters. The contemporary engraving by David Allan shows the inner quadrangle of the University with an exhibition of pictures in the open air. This was held on 22nd September, 1761, to celebrate the coronation of George III.—an event which probably explains the bonfire which must have caused some concern to the exhibitors. There would appear to be nothing new in the matter of crowds which attend special art exhibitions in our day, to judge from the Foulis records : "All the gates were thrown open, and multitudes of every description from the city and country adjacent crowded to see them."

The Academy had among its students, in addition to David Allan, William Cochran, Alexander Runciman and James Tassie, the latter famous for his portrait medallions of his notable contemporaries. Through its productions and the influences exercised by artists trained in the Academy the Foulis experiment, notwithstanding the final disaster must be marked as a notable event in the University's history. The pictures in the Hunterian Collection—some of them are internationally famous, e.g. the three Chardins

—would not have been there but for William Hunter's interest in the Fine Arts, an interest almost certainly created by the Foulis brothers. Hunter's association with the Royal Academy of which he was Professor of Anatomy, brought him into contact with Sir Joshua Reynolds the first president, and there is evidence of other associations with artistic and literary circles in London. For example, in the University Library there is a receipt for five shillings from Hogarth to William Hunter for the former's "Analysis of Beauty." It is more than likely that his reputation as a connoisseur was acquired in London but the starting point was in Glasgow.

As we come forward into the nineteenth century there is not much evidence of a University interest in the Arts. Indeed, when the old College buildings in the High Street were abandoned (and the new University was built on Gilmorehill) those responsible seemed to have known or cared little or nothing for architectural values. To-day, among knowledgable people, the question constantly arises, " What would ' Greek ' Thomson have made of such a great site and of such a grand opportunity?" William Power, in " The World Unvisited," commenting on the astonishing negligence in failing to engage the Glasgow architect Alexander Thomson, then at the height of his powers, and who is now acknowledged as a genius, says this : " To the London shop the University went therefore : and the result is the monument of dullness, disharmony and pretentious ineffectiveness that sprawls over the crest of Gilmorehill like a dismantled cargo steamer on the crest of a green wave." Certainly the surrender to the fashion of bogus Gothic architecture was a sad mistake, which may have influenced the equally lamentable conclusions which led to the formidable chunk of masonry known as " The Art Gallery."

In the eighties the Glasgow School of Painters brought

considerable renown to the city and in various ways re-
established the University's contacts with the Fine Arts.
Among its activities was " *The Scottish Art Review*," a
publication which had in view ". The furtherance of a
knowledge and a love of that aspect of divine truth which
it is the privilege of Art to present to men." Principal
Caird was one of his contributors. His essay " Progres-
siveness in Art " is of special interest today in the light of
current theories in art education and criticism—especially
with regard to Child Art and the modern movement. Here
is what the principal of the University wrote in 1888 :

" If it be the function of art to idealise the world, the
child is often an unconscious artist; for, out of the
common matter-of-fact world of sense and sight, it
creates a new and brighter World, or sheds around the
real World an atmosphere in which ordinary objects and
appearances are transformed, refracted, recombined."

and

"Art is but one of the ways in which the thought and
culture, the spirit of an age expresses itself. It is, in
one sense, the depository of its richest intuitions, its
deepest reflections, its purest aspirations. If man
progresses therefore art must progress."

One of the editors who tried, in vain, to continue the
Scottish Art Review as a going concern was James Mavor,
an uncle of O. H. Mavor (James Bridie). Other University
connections with the Glasgow School were maintained
though individual artists such as Sir James Guthrie and E.
A. Walton, father of Professor John Walton who holds the
Regius chair of Botany. E. A. Walton was a near neighbour of Whistler in Chelsea, and has recorded the latter's
unfeigned delight when the University intimated its
decision to award. him an LL.D. That was in 1903.
Before then, in 1891, Walton had taken a leading part
along with other members of the Glasgow Art Club, in

urging the Corporation to acquire Whistler's portrait of Carlyle. These two events may have led to a third, viz. the presentation to the University in 1936 of paintings, etchings and personal memorials of Whistler by his sister-in-law, Miss Birnie Philip.

The link with the Walton family is maintained in Professor Walton's honorary post as Curator of the Fine Art Collections in the Hunterian Museum, the Catalogue of which has been compiled by Mrs. Walton.

When the late Dr. James McCallum gifted his comprehensive collection of prints and drawings, the University became the possessor of a unique range of works by the great masters in the graphic arts and provision has been made to ensure that gaps can be filled as opportunities arise.

Two important tasks remain to be completed before it can be said that the University is able to offer the full liberal education implicit in its function. The first, a department devoted to the study of the history and appreciation of the Fine Arts, is on the way. The appointment of Mr. McLaren Young to a lectureship in Fine Arts marks a forward step which has already brought results in some interesting discoveries on the attributions of paintings in the Hunter Collection. The second, a new and fully equipped Art Gallery is included in the new building programme. It will then be possible to display adequately works of art, hitherto enjoyed chiefly by specialists, privileged and surprised visitors. We are quite uninformed on the matter of priorities but we know that the Principal is more than sympathetic and is anxious to have the University play a fuller part in developing all the Arts as an integral part of University Education. Music is well established. The pictorial arts are next and, who knows, drama may yet be in the running. Sir Hector Hetherington, surrounded as he must be with the noise of builders and the bleating of persistent planners, may deplore the habit history has of repeating itself. In the *Letters and Journals* of Rober Baillie (1599-1662) there is a peevish complaint against Patrick Gillespie the principal, of whom it is said (1658) : " Mr. Gillespie's work is building and pleas : with the din of masons, wrights, carters, smiths we are vexed every day."—but, later on, there is this : " Upon these foundations are our palaces builded. . . . "

Through reconstruction and extension the University still says " Draw near unto me ye unlearned and dwell in the house of learning." It is also becoming aware of the truth that "The wisdom of a learned man cometh by opportunity of leisure." One fine day we shall know how to make full use of vacations. Then the Arts will come into their own.

G

THE DIALECTIC SOCIETY

By James Willocks

(Vice-President of the Society and Clerk of the House.)

For five hundred years the Dialectic Society has been a University within a University. In this article the Society's scholarly Vice-President traces its history from the earliest days. Educated at Hutchesons' Grammar School, James Willocks is a fifth year medical student and a former President of the Conservative Club but his interests are not only in the hospitals and the Debating Hall as this article will show.

The Dialectic is getting older every year. This statement is less trite than it seems, for the Dialectic gets older in a way peculiar to itself; not only does it add on years in the normal way of all mortal things, but its presidents discover from time to time that it was founded at an earlier date than they had previously supposed, so that for the past few years they have announced that the Dialectic is older than the University itself, adding, in a complacent and amiable cliché, that its origin is lost in the mists of antiquity. But, alas, Clio is a sterner mistress than whatever muse is served by our fertile-brained presidents, and the historian must disregard this agreeable legend. Yet it does contain a grain of truth, for the dialectic spirit can be traced back beyond the founding of Universities, and, in Glasgow, our own Dialectic Society had many predecessors.

Probably the earliest of them had its origin in one of those tavern gatherings of medieval students (intellectually brilliant even if morally reprobate) celebrated in the *Carmina Burana*—

> *Scyphi crebro repetiti*
> *non dormiant*
> *Et sermones inauditi*
> *prosiliant.*

The Middle Ages were the great years of dialectic, of formal disputation in the Aristotelian manner, of silver-tongued logicians from Peter Abelard to Pico della Mirandola, and in such an intellectual atmosphere a students' dialectic society at a new University was a natural growth bound to flourish. We may assume that, in some form or other, the dialectic tradition survived the storms of the Reformation, and threw up some exotic blooms in the metaphysical jungle of Calvinism in those centuries when even the labourer at the plough, having no other spare-time occupation, made himself adept in theological argument.

In the early years of the eighteenth century, several clubs or debating societies were formed amongst the students. They all had high-sounding names—the Trinampherian Club, the Anticappadocian Club, and the Eleutherian Club, which was composed of students "who affected to be persons of bright parts."

'Jupiter' Carlyle, when a student at Glasgow in 1743-45, was a member of a literary club which met in the porter's lodge at the College, and of another club which " met in Mr. Dugald's tavern near the Cross, weekly, and admitted a mixture of young gentlemen not intended for the study of theology." There they regaled themselves with punch, beefsteak and pancakes, the charge to each member seldom exceeding 1/- a night.

In 1768 there were two student clubs, the General Society, which was a debating club, and the Parliament of Oceana—the parliament of a fictitious republic; thus these two societies performed the functions later fulfilled by the Dialectic Society—debating on general subjects, and parliamentary debating.

The Dialectic Society is mentioned by name for the first time in 1776, when it was one of the three students' societies, the others being the Eclectic and the Academic. Its meetings were held in the college rooms, and were well attended by students and visitors, " and sometimes the professors graced the ingenuous youths with their presence and encouraged to diligence."

After some years, however, the society (at least, under the name of " Dialectic ") disappears from view, being replaced by the College Debating Club and others, but in 1862 it re-appears in strength, like the river Alpheus after its passage through the caverns underground. It was then that the present Dialectic Society was founded. Membership was at first confined to students in the classes of Logic, Moral Philosophy and Natural Philosophy, and to divinity students who had passed through these classes, and in that year there were 45 members. The records of the Society's earlier years did not survive the transition from the Old College to Gilmorehill, but I have before me, as I write, the minute books of the Society from 1879.

From the stained and dog-eared pages of the Victorian volumes, the Dialectic emerges as the premier Society of the University, illustrious and unchallenged. In 1889 the membership reached a record of 811; the opening address of the year was given to a large and distinguished audience in the Bute Hall by the Duke of Argyll on "The fallacies due to neglected elements"; the Society returned two members to the S.R.C (which, indeed, it had helped to found) and was about to give a second donation to the infant Students' Union—the first donation of £20 having been given in 1885, when the Union was founded. It was then the custom to elect the honorary president from the staff, and the office was held by eminent scholars like Nichol, Lushington, Jebb and Bradley, and by Sir William Tennant Gairdner, perhaps the most distinguished of the humanist physicians of the late Victorian era.

Prominent among the student members were Cosmo Lang, later Archbishop of Canterbury and Robert Horne, later Chancellor of the Exchequer, who for many years presented the prize for the Dialectic freshers' competition.

A notable feature of those spacious days was the Annual Dinner. In 1886, the Dinner was held in the Grand Hotel, Charing Cross, with Professor R. C. Jebb in the chair; the menu included—ox-tail or Palestine soup, cod with oyster sauce, filets maitre d'hotel, mutton cutlets, saute of kidneys, pigeons and peas, sirloin of beef, haunch of mutton, roast chickens, boiled capons, Wiltshire ham, tongue, Chancellor pudding, tart, souffle, jelly, creams, stewed fruit and (magnificently!) etc.

The chairman proposed the toasts of the Queen; the Prince and Princess of Wales and the other members of the Royal Family; the Navy, Army and Reserve Forces, and the toast of the Society, to which last reply was made by the President, Mr. C. S. Horne, who was acting as croupier. Professor W. T. Gairdner replied to the toast of the University, and (we presume) a good time was had by all.

But our grandfathers combined such Gargantuan jollifications with intellectual pabulum for which few of our present students would have either strength or inclination.

The meetings were opened with prayer, and matters of the highest import were often discussed. Subjects such as " That the Church of Scotland be disestablished " and " Is man a fallen creature? " took their turn with literary and with political subjects some of whose titles sound strangely modern—" That the land should be nationalised " and " That the House of Lords be abolished." Besides discussing general political topics, the Society had several " parliamentary nights " in the year, and this custom survives in an attenuated form when the President of the Dialectic takes the chair at one of the regular Union Parliamentary Debates. Indeed, in 1887 there was an attempt to convert the Dialectic into a Parliamentary Debating Society, but better counsels prevailed, and the breadth of the Constitution remained unimpaired. Distinguished lecturers, including Professors Jebb, Latta, Saintsbury, John Stuart Blackie, Gilbert Murray and Edward Caird (later Master of Baliol), also frequently addressed the Society.

But high seriousness, though paramount, was not permanent, and towards the end of the century a more frivolous note creeps into the subjects discussed, which included—" That the Scotch (*sic*) character is repulsive," " Lawyers and Liars," and " That barmaids be abolished."

In 1891, Professor Tyndall (known to Science students by the " Tyndall Effect ") presented the Society with its magnificent Mace, which the Secretary, in his report, said " added materially to the dignity of the proceedings." The Secretary also announced that " The Board has had the pleasure of lending the Mace to the University Union on the occasions of the Union Debates "—a custom still in force.

In 1892 the first joint debate with Queen Margaret College Debating Society took place, the subject being " That Rudyard Kipling is entitled to a place in literature." Disaster almost overtook this bold venture, for the Vice-President of Queen Margaret College had intimated to the ladies that "in view of the present delicate position of the College "—its members not being matriculated students—the proposed debate could not take place ; but it was finally conceded that the ladies should attend but not speak, their papers being read by members of the Dialectic Society.

The fears of the Queen Margaret College Authorities had evidently been groundless, for they wrote later to thank the Dialectic Society for " the manner of their entertainment " at the joint debate.

However, in the 'nineties, there were signs of decline in the Society. In the session 1896-97 the membership had fallen to 139, and the Secretary in his annual report said that this was due partly to the institution of the S.R.C. (where many of the matters previously discussed at the Dialectic were now thrashed out) and partly to the growth of other societies, but that the real cause lay in " an utter absence of all Academic Esprit de Corps." " This result," he continued, "would seem to spring largely from the new Regulations for Degrees, which have left men no time to do anything but cram."

A new feature which did much to restore the waning fortunes of the Society was the " Trial by Jury " which was introduced for the first time in 1896, when it was the event of the session, and was repeated with great success in the following years, one of the most sensational cases being the breach of promise action of " Mantrap v. McSoftey " in 1904.

The Secretary's report for 1905 ends on a note of calm confidence, and the Society certainly remained lively and resilient during the Edwardian (or, for Glasgow students, the Elliot-Mavor) era; but here I am faced with another hiatus in my evidence, for several of the minute books, in the careless irreverent way that minute books of student societies have, have vanished.

From other sources we learn that, although the attendance at ordinary meetings was regrettably small, the public lectures which were addressed by Sir Walter Raleigh, Sir Sidney Lee and Hilaire Belloc, among others, continued popular, and at the jubilee dinner on March 1st the President declared that the Society had had fifty years of unbroken success.

Broken, however, the tradition of the Society soon was by the Great War of 1914-18, when it fell completely into abeyance.

In 1919 the Society was resuscitated due to the energies of the Secretary, Mr. E. W. M. Heddle, and at the opening meeting Professor Phillimore remarked that " the simplest way to relieve an overloaded brain is to gather together a few friends and make an audience of them; and in a Dialectic Society the sacrifice is equitably distributed."

The " Few Friends " rapidly grew, and by 1922 the Dialectic had been restored to something like its old strength with a membership of 661.   But despite this apparent prosperity it is discouraging to see the Dialectic angling for popular support so blatantly as it did in the 'twenties by holding " Royal Commissions " to enquire into the state of the S.R.C., the Union, Charities Week, the Political Clubs, G.U.M., and any and every University activity.

Other details are more pleasing.   The Professors' Debate was introduced as an annual feature, was a great success, and has remained so ever since, and in 1921 a " Trial by Jury," which raised a considerable sum of money for the Infirmaries, was held in the Bute Hall. Encouraged by this success, the Society decided ten years later to produce a play, and Sheridan's " The Critic " was performed in the Lyric Theatre in April, 1931, but this involved the Dialectic in a financial crisis of the first magnitude from which it never has recovered.

In March 1933 there was a debate—in imitation of the famous Oxford motion—on the subject " That this House is prepared to fight for King and Country." Mr. Hector McNeil, who writes elsewhere in this volume, was one of the leading speakers, and the attendance throughout the debate was a record one, there never being less than 1,500 persons present. The motion was defeated by 66 votes, and a correspondence in the press which lasted for two months followed on the debate.

The prosperity of the Society must not be judged by this sensational debate, for the attendance at ordinary meetings averaged about twenty, and funds were low.

Subjects dealing with disarmament, Fascism and the possibility of a future war appear with ominous frequency in the minutes. These later minute books are less interesting than the earlier ones, for the old zest and the old sense of importance are gone; no longer are the pages adorned with copies of all the posters issued by the Society, and with colourful menu cards for the annual dinner; no longer do we read that " The President was accompanied on the platform by the Principal and members of the Senate, including . . ." for the Society's connection with the University Authorities, which had been maintained by its Honorary Presidents, was now much less close. The office of Honorary President was now usually filled by someone outside the University— chiefly by a succession of popular authors including Ian Hay, James Bridie, John Buchan, J. B. Priestley, Hugh Walpole and Eric Linklater.

At the Annual General Meeting in 1937 there was talk of disbanding the Society, but the meeting proved so lively that a motion " That an Annual General Meeting should be held at least once a month " was carried—although not into practice.

In 1939 the Dialectic was again in sad plight, but was saved by the amalgamation with Queen Margaret Union Debating Society. To this timely union with the ladies the Society probably owes not only such prosperity as it now has, but its very existence.

The recent war dealt more kindly with the Society than did the previous one, and continuity was preserved. Although no evening meetings were held, afternoon War commentaries proved popular, and in October, 1941 there was held for the first time the Political Symposium which has remained one of the best attended events of the session.

Last year the Society had a membership of 140, and particularly attractive subjects recently discussed were—" That women be disfranchised," " That co-education is no education " and " That the loss of the human tail was an unmitigated disaster."

The history of the Dialectic is not just a record of the way some of the students at the University spent some of their spare time. It is a history of literary, philosophical and political thought. In its debates have been mirrored all the great trends of the past nine decades—the old Scottish passion for metaphysics, the political enthusiasms of the greatest period in our parliamentary history, the blasé and faded decadence of the 'nineties, the birth of Socialism, the confident Imperialism of the Edwardian age and all the tortured strivings of the last two generations. All this may sound pretentious, but it is none the less true.

Finally, we must remember this : the Dialectic was an active and flourishing body before the Union or the S.R.C. were even conceived; it is the doyen of all our clubs, and remains a living force in the corporate life of the University.

THE SLIDE THAT JAMMED.

By ART STUDENT.

Glasgow University, like all old and changing institutions, is not without its self consciousness and introspection. Art Student, a student of one of the extra-mural colleges, describes us as others see us—a description which gives some food for thought.

"ART School," the University students decide as a young beard appears at the end of the tram queue. Staggering under something approaching his own weight in boards, boxes, bags and bulges this hirsute one can be immediately identified as an art student. Not for him the neat despatch case or the slim text book under the arm, the fountain pen clip and impeccable tie. T-squares and Double Elephant drawing boards make him difficult to ignore on the crowded transports, rolls of paper protrude from the folds of his green and black scarf and tin-foil, balls of wool and hog-hair brushes extrude from every nook and cranny of his coat. His last tram-ticket is still between his teeth.

"Art School," the American visitor informs the surprised Glaswegian as he points up the hill from Sauchiehall Street to the back of Charles Rennie Mackintosh's grey masterpiece of steel and concrete. Built on the highest peak of the Garnet Drumlins this solid, dreaming fortress casts its eye-rim up towards the sky and has all Glasgow, the Regal Cinema and the Campsie Hills on the perimeter of its

vision   "Oh, I thought that was the Macalpine Nursing
Home," murmurs the interested native.

"Now for Glasgow University," says the architecture
lecturer in the Charles Rennie Mackintosh lecture theatre.
A hush falls over the assembled students.   "Erected on
Gilmorehill in the 1870's, Gothic in detail, Renaissance in
plan."   The silence congeals as the ghost of a Scottish neo-
Gothic architecture hangs on the screen, then a shiver
rattles the hard dry benches.   A momentary shiver this,
unlike the one which moans eternally among the grim, dark
cloisters of the University. Thousands of neat undergraduates move like ants through the vast, admired cata-
combs which lie beyond the Union and Pearce Lodge.   In
anguish the spirit of Charles Rennie Mackintosh beats
within the Art School heating pipes.   The slide in the
epidiascope jams.

*   *   *

"What do you think of the University? "   I whisper in
the dark to the back benchers.   This is not idle curiosity. I
have been asked to find out.

" My brother's there," says a huddle in the corner.

" Mine's got the cramps from re-sits," says another.

" It's either that or intellectual indigestion, isn't it? "

There is a pause of agreement while the University slide
re-appears on the screen, this time upside down.

"But there are a great many fine people up there," I try
to hold their attention as they begin to applaud the sight
before them.

" Oh yes, couldn't do without them."

The shape of the upturned University is quite interesting.
So few people have the time to appreciate things from
more than one angle.   There are those, too, who are
subjected to so many opinions from books as to the true
appearance of things, that they feel as informed as though
they had used their own mind's eye.

" Book learning's a very second-hand way of getting experience," says a thoughtful shape at my side. It's all right as a supplement to personal investigation but the danger of too much too soon is that you never learn to stand on your own feet at all. Your material may be built up as logically and precisely as you like, but what use is that if you're building on vague assumption and not on belief."

" Bernard Shaw says fine art is the only teacher except torture," I offer, having just acquired Herbert Read's " Education through Art."

"Fine Art can be torture too," he replies, "if you happen to be in the business."

We speak very quietly indeed. Lecturers at the Art School come to expect an orderly audience. There seems little desire among this one for individual self-expression in the possible form of back-chat, mass yodelling, and whistling. The true art student expresses himself in his work all the time so has little need for sporadic outbursts. Nor does he rid himself of inhibitions at set times as University students may do, every year, on the wall designs for Daft Friday.

I nudge my neighbour again. " I like the University, don't you.? " He nods vigorously. " Oh yes, but it's a pity we don't know the first thing about one another."

This makes me think of a recent scene during coffee break. A wild-eyed fellow in a floral shirt was banging his fist on the table and shouting about the University graduate. " The so-called professional man is the artist's most virulent and uninformed critic. He's above criticism himself, he thinks, because he knows ten known facts out of ten. But does he hesitate to criticise the creative artist for trying to gain a few footholds in an infinity of experience? Not him. He just says, 'I don't know much about art, mind you, but I know what I like! ' Then he shows you. ' *The Hopeless Dawn.*' "

Is the Art School then the only haven of the misunderstood and the isolated few? So the chap in the Refectory seemed to think.

"Who is that fellow with the wild eyes and the floral shirt," I nudge my friend again. " What section does he work in?"

He rather wearily removes his attention from a bird's eye view of the University and answers. " He isn't an art student at all, just vaguely connected by poetry to some amateur theatrical company. He comes up for a cup of tea because it's cheap."

Oh for a cup of tea now! But why is the original University slide again on the screen, still upside down? What is this piece of information we are being offered? The first art school in Glasgow was started by the first University printer. Everybody gasps. We didn't think the University ever knew we existed, except on Charities Day.

Present day art students are given the false impression that the only interest shown towards the Art School by University undergraduates is confined to a basement window through which surprise entry may sometimes be made to the Christmas Art Ball.

But Glasgow Universtiy was founded almost five hundred years ago, we are being told. Already informed of this well ahead of my colleagues, I tap the shoulder of the chap in front of me.

" What do you think of the Fifth Centenary?" I whisper.

He works it out on his hands. 1451. He turns round with some excitement. That was the year before Leonardo da Vinci was born. Could not a double celebration be arranged? Was this not an opportunity to bring art and science together, to make a plea for more liberal education?

What greater inspiration could the seeker for universal knowledge find than Leonardo? Although the lack of a combustion engine prevented him from inventing the first aeroplane, there was very little he did not know about mathematics, engineering, biology, geology, botany, astronomy, anatomy, grammar, music, sculpture, drawing and painting, not to mention psychology.

Five hundred years of scientific research certainly mounts up. Nowadays a whole lifetime may be spent in the study of one particular type of bug which may be picked off the back of another type of bug, this being the place we are told, where bugs are most commonly situated.

"But no Leonarda ever goes to a University these days," I am informed by my most thoughtful friend. "Modern University study means research, clarification, analysis and memory training. It has nothing to do with the development of the creative, original side of human nature."

The last word on the matter is spoken by a very young girl who has been listening to us from behind.

"I don't think you know what you're talking about," she says. "The University must be full of poets, playwrights, composers and novelists, all of them geniuses. Look at the number of them who come out every year as MASTERS of Arts."

The University slide leaps off the screen for the last time.

THE OLD COLLEGE

By Elspeth Gallie, M.A.

Elspeth Gallie has only recently left Gilmorehill where she was a well known figure in Student life. She has been Debates Convener for Queen Margaret Union, Q.M. President, S.R.C. and Q.M. President of the Dialectic Society. She is now Curator of the Old Glasgow Museum, the People's Palace on Glasgow Green. That the Old College was one of the most important buildings of old Glasgow is a fact often overlooked. Miss Gallie shows in the following pages just how important that building was.

GLASGOW in the past, it is said, was famous for three things—the Cathedral, the Clyde, and the College.

Certainly, early Glasgow, for long enough a collection of clergymen's houses, clustered round the Church, owed its existence to the Cathedral, for there was a Church on the Molendinar before there was a Glasgow. There was also a river, and the town could never have developed as it did without it. There is considerable truth in the cliché that Glasgow made the Clyde and the Clyde made Glasgow, and just as the Clyde is the symbol of Glasgow today, so the Cathedral was the symbol of the medieval city.

And what of the College, you might ask ? It cannot be said to be symbolic of one special period in Glasgow's history, although architecturally it belongs to the Glasgow of the merchants. It was the greatest gift of medieval to modern Glasgow, and as such is part and parcel of the city's history. From its site in the High Street, it has seen Glasgow as a medieval burgh, as a prosperous little trading township, and as a huge industrial city, itself unchanging, comparatively speaking, in a changing world. When the scene around it had changed rather too much, the College, following the trend of the city, moved west.

It is not easy for us today to picture the setting of the Old College. Even in the seventeenth century, when the Old College building was replacing the remains of the New Pedagogy, Glasgow had not changed a great deal from the burgh of the Middle Ages. It was still little more than one main street, crossed at intervals by two others. The Clyde, famous for its trout and its salmon, was its southern boundary, and the Cathedral was its northern. Beyond were only the wide open spaces. Between the two, climbed the High Street, somewhat steeper than today, crossed near the river by the Trongate and the Gallowgate, and near the Cathedral by the Rottenrow and the Drygate. The High Street was Glasgow and in the High Street stood the College, the fairest sight, we are told, between the Cathedral and the Cross. This was no small tribute, for the Glasgow of the 17th and 18th centuries had a high reputation for the beauty of its buildings. John Macky, in 1723, declared with extreme enthusiasm that " Glasgow is the beautifullest little city I have seen in Britain." Another visitor, John Ray, wrote in 1662, that Glasgow was " fair, large and well built . . . somewhat like unto Oxford." What better setting, therefore, could one wish for a College ? Even the Pope, Nicholas V. thought so, though he had heard of it only by hearsay, and affirmed in the Bull of Foundation " that it was a place well suited and

H

adapted to that purpose on account of the healthiness of
the climate, of the plenty of victuals, and of everything
necessary for the use of man."

There was a University on the same site on the east side
of the High Street, since Lord Hamilton's grant of
property was gratefully received in 1460, though the
erection of the building, half new, half restored which
we now know as the Old College, was not begun
systematically till 1632. The period of the Old College,
however, marked a turn in the fortunes of the little
University, which had not hitherto had too happy a
career. Indeed by the time of Queen Mary we read that
it " appearit rather to be the Decay of ane University, nor
onyways to be reckonit ane established foundation."

This state of affairs was not due only to the lack of
college buildings. There was also a dearth of young
students, and early lists reveal that the student population
consisted mainly of clerics, of canons, vicars, rectors,
priests, abbots, monks, who enrolled partly to give a
fillip to the struggling venture, and partly, no doubt, to
enjoy the privileges of being a student. The University's
fortunes became more stabilised with the turn of the 16th
century and the process of building and renovation which
produced the Old College.

I shall not attempt here to give a complete word-picture
of the Old College. For one thing, Slezer's engraving
depicts it far more effectively. For another, it would be
difficult to do so, since it was built over a considerable
period of time, in bits and pieces, here a staircase, there a
court, now a steeple, then a library, and so on. Its
characteristics, we are told, are those of " Heriots hospital
and other Scotch erections of the time." It had two courts
outer and inner, and a square steeple. Beyond the inner
court were the College gardens, well furnished, we are
told, with fruit trees and pot herbs and countless hedges,

The Colledge of Glasgow

SLEZER'S VIEW

where the Masters and selected students were allowed to walk. Democracy being then just a shadow of its future self, only the sons of the nobility were given the keys of the garden gate! Later a third court was built to provide sorely needed houses for the Professors, who had long been feeling the shortage.

Though thought impressive at the time, it was not a large building—334 feet long by 141 feet broad. Perhaps the best idea of its relative size can be given by a comparison of the Pearce Lodge gateway (the gateway to the Old College) with its present-day surroundings.

So picture, if you can, the College in its early, almost rural setting. Ours was a quiet town in the 17th century, and the College a peaceful and pleasant place where the diligent could pursue uninterrupted studies. Behind the gardens the Molendinar gurgled on its way to join the Clyde. The silence and the peace would be broken perhaps, by the chirping of the birds in the College gardens, or by the Cathedral bells, or perhaps by the Town-herd's horn as he gathered his cows together in the High Street. The cows, on their morning pilgrimage down the High Street past the Trongate and up the Cow Lone (Queen Street) to the green pastures of what is now George Square, were a daily sight for any student, and must have added the final pastoral touch to the scene. They came back the same way in the evening, but it was ulikely that the student, even if he cared enough, would see them, since he would have to be in bed by then.

Such was the College; but the earliest conception of a University was that of a group of people, rather than of a place, and we cannot, in speaking of the Old College, with impunity omit to mention the students.

Though not as numerous as they are today, they made their mark and enjoyed their existence. They were cabbin'd, cribbed and confined in a manner incredible to

the present-day Glasgow student, but they had their
privileges too (rent-free rooms, for example being a bless-
ing not to be sneezed at). Life, though, was not by any
means roses all the way. They rose at dawn and any
student caught dozing at 5 a.m. received from the Principal's own hand a public whipping, witnessed and enjoyed
by the entire College. O tempora, O mores! With the
passing of the centuries, the wheel has turned full cycle,
and 5 a.m. by present custom, it is not so much the hour
for leaving one's bed as the hour for going into it.

At the same time, woe to the delinquent not in bed by 9
p.m. in winter (relaxed to 10 p.m. in summer), for the Professors went round, birch in hand, to make sure that the
College rules were being obeyed. There were other rules
of course, of which we will mention only a few, since their
name was legion. While " Gouffe, Archerie, and lyke
sports " were encouraged, all " Dicing, Billiards, and the
indecent exercise of Bathing " were strictly forbidden. The
more flagrant offences were those of wearing swords,
of robbing the College orchards, and of " being found
drinking in an ale house with some touns people at 11
of the clock at night." The worst crime of all was that
of using one's mother tongue, for Latin was not only used
for lecturing, it was the recognised means of communication for students during College hours, even when talking
to the servants, and any *lapsus linguae* was severely
punished. A very common practical joke was that of
handing in to the Cathedral the name of a fellow-student,
to be publicly prayed for at the next service. Such
solicitude blossomed like a flower, and became so wide-
spread that it had to be suppressed with a heavy hand.

There were other things the student must not do. An
enactment enjoins that " any student who should meet any
one of the Professors in the streets without seeking to avoid
his glance, or even play any game in his presence, should

be subject to severe corporal punishment. If it so happened that such a meeting took place in a narrow thoroughfare, where escape was impossible, the student was permitted to hold both his hands in front of his face and pretend not to see his superior." This practice was in vogue in the days of the Auld and New Pedagogies and was known as " shirking."

Nor were the regulations for the students alone. It was decreed that " inasmuch as women are vain, frivolous, and gifted with an exceeding great gift of Words, and by their Blandishments are apt at times to distract the minds even of grave Professors, wherefore these latter are strictly counselled not to marry : but in the event of their being compelled by untoward Force of Circumstances to choose between two Evils, they are prohibited, on pain of removal from their Chairs from bringing their Better-halves within the College walls."

There is a great deal more which could be said about the Old College and its famous men, but as this is a mere article and not a concise history of the University, I am somewhat restricted.

It is only right, however, to mention before closing, some of the benefactors who made the growth, indeed, the existence of the Old College possible. I say some, because the list is a very long one. There was Queen Mary with her bursaries for five poor youths, in the early and difficult days of Pedagogies. There was Andrew Melville, whose lectures made Glasgow College so famous that students even came from St. Andrews to hear them. And there was the most famous, perhaps, of them all, Zachary Boyd of the Barony. It is partly due to him that the decayed buildings of the University were restored and rebuilt in the 17th century into the Old College. An article therefore, on the Old College would scarcely be complete without some account of him. This " fantastick old gentleman," as

Principal Baillie dubbs him was, in addition to being Minister of the Barony from 1623 to 1654, thrice Dean of the Faculty and thrice Rector. He was famed for his strong convictions and even stronger personality. When Cromwell in the role of conqueror, came to Glasgow in 1650 with his Ironsides, he attended Sunday worship in the High Kirk. Zachary was in the pulpit at the time, and nothing daunted by the new element in his congregation, gave out to be sung the 79th psalm, beginning :

> " O God, the heathen enter'd have
> Into thine heritage; by them
> Defiled is thy house; in heaps
> They laid Jerusalem."

He then took as his text the 8th chapter of Daniel, drawing an unmistakeable comparison between the rough he-goat and the Lord Protector. How Cromwell got his own back is, of course, another story.

When he died, he left £20,000 Scots " for the use of the said college," and the University, in gratitude for his munificence placed a stone bust of the benefactor in a niche under the College tower, but did not carry out the condition of the bequest, which was that it should publish all his literary works. This negligence may well have been due to respect for his memory. While his prose was in no way remarkable, his poetry undoubtedly was. In his poetry he confined himself to religious subjects and was popularly supposed to have turned the whole Bible into verse, though this belief is by no means well founded. Originals are few, however, and parodies and burlesques are many, so that it is difficult to divide the true from the false. The following gems are attributed, though, by many to him :

> " And Jacob made for his wee Josie,
> A tartan Coat to keep him cosie,
> And what for na, ther was nae harm,
> To keep the lad baith saft and warm."

also :

"There was a man called Job, dwelt in the Land of Uz;
He had a good gift of the Gob, the same case happen us."

His bust, we are glad to say, was removed along with the famous Lion and Unicorn stair to Gilmorehill when the Railway Company took over the site in High Street, and is one of the few physical links with the Old College.

Edinburgh still has its Old College quadrangle; St. Andrews has its St. Mary's and its St. Salvator's, and Aberdeen has Kings. It seems a pity that we in Glasgow have left only a gateway, a statue, and a stair. Mercifully a University is composed not merely of buildings but of people. Thus, while the factors of time and space do influence it, they are merely factors. A University is too intangible a thing to be dependent on time or place or to be measured accurately in their terms. Under these conditions we can prophesy with safety that Glasgow College, wherever she may be placed, should have a future ahead as rich as the past that lies behind her.

UNION DEBATES

By The Right Honourable HECTOR McNEIL, M.P.

*The Right Honourable Hector McNeil, M.P. was
a student in the Faculty of Arts. He was Union Convener of Debates and toured the U.S.A. and Canada
with a British Universities Debating team. In 1941
he was elected Member of Parliament for Greenock,
a seat which he has held ever since. He was the
British delegate to the United Nations from 1946 to
1949 and is now Secretary of State for Scotland. In
this article he gives his impressions of debating in the
Union he knew so well.*

It is flattering but unjust that I should be invited to
write about the Union debates. There are those who can
remember when the giants mouthed their way around.
This debating business began in the Union, as far as I can
read, less than 70 years ago. There must be some of those
mighty men in whom the fire still burns brightly. One of
the giants should have written of the Union debates in the
days when all were giants.

Round about 1885 they began debating in the Glasgow
University Union. I expect that that is scarcely accurate.
I suppose Glasgow men must always have debated somewhere; but around 1885 it became a religion. It is
probable that the Union itself was the outcome of debate;

so the Union was raised as a temple to Demos. For on the
other side of the century Glasgow men debated for the
good but insufficient reason that they wanted to debate.
Debates for them, were not squalid engagements, demand-
ing the clarification of some proposition, or much worse,
insisting that there should be some outcome to the talking.
Words were then as plentiful as whisky—and as satisfactory. And whisky was then five shillings a bottle.

By the time I came to the Union, the rot had set in.
Morality, or responsibility, or a political viewpoint, was
expected. Rhetoric, that delightful but heady wine, was
not enough. A speech was a failure unless someone
sweated profusely before it was made and many, more
profusely, after its delivery.

The sub-editors to whom I was afterwards apprenticed,
had a share in the blame. They called every other speech
a " clarion call," and so the confusion set in. People
thought that speeches build walls. The men of 1885 knew
better. They knew that speeches issued not from clarions
but from trumpets, and that the Good Lord vouchsafed
an occasional miracle to hearten and to stimulate the
talkers not by raising the walls of a new Jerusalem in the
wake of a speech, but by letting tumble down now and
then the walls of an old Jericho.

But by 1930 we were a timid and a pigmied crowd,
solemn and self-conscious. There were one or two—like
the great Togo O'Hear—who could defend, and would
defend, any proposition with eloquence and ingenuity and
something that sounded like passion, for no other reason
than that they liked talking well, and knew that they could
talk well. They were, however, rare. There were no
heroes like C. E. Montague who put the world right from
one point of view, and crossed the street to put it wrong
from the other point of view as a daily performance and a
nightly miracle and for the most part, we were garrulous

Gradgrinds. I made my first speech on coal. I knew about coal. I knew the output; the number of men employed; the wages they received; the prices realised; the gross amount of royalties. And all the Royal Commissions. The G.U.M, with that tolerance and graciousness it always extended toward maiden speakers said that " it was a pity that Mr. McNeil had forgotten his bloody soapbox!" This was, of course, unjust as well as inaccurate. I took it with me. It has been with me ever since.

But there we were—the pigmies after the giants, consumed, not by passion, but possessed by fact. Argument was our business, instead of rhetoric being our delight. Words for us were not for sale, and certainly were not for murder. I, like the many, formed then the ungainly habit of believing that action should follow words. It has been for me a rich and constant source of disappointment, and I console myself by thinking that my disappointment will be even greater if, and when, I find myself on the Opposition benches. Sometimes, in my more sombre moments, I conclude that this change is or was to be expected. Glasgow University in all its massive greatness, must reflect the Clydeside if it is to be itself. The rollicking expansive days of the 1880's must have sent to the Union rollicking and braggart lads. By 1930, expansion was not quite so noticeable and even the most irresponsible of us must occasionally have noticed the shadows. At any rate, we were then all branded, and in all the quarters of this closing world, I have met men from that period of the Union, all displaying this sombre belief in the value of the spoken word. Some, of course, have become even more unbelievably solemn than others. These are the fellows who have taken to writing comedies for the stage. Two who fought and dared to be light-hearted in these days, Roger McDougal and Alan Mackinnon, could not escape this mourning destiny. They wrote comedies for the screen.

Worst of all, that dear and engaging jester, Andrew Ewart, has written comedies for the radio.

I'm inclined to the belief that the depressing seriousness of the modern comedy is due to this heavy responsibility which seeped into every speaker in the Union in my time, and doubtless was mirrored in the debates of all the contemporary Unions. Words apparently still matter; are still the language of action, even when they are supposed to be humorous.

Other fellows, of a more buoyant frame of mind, went into the Ministry of the Church of Scotland, where, despite all the blandishments of high church leaders, they persist in using their own sincere words in the form of prayers and exhortations, continuing to believe that miracles may yet follow. Then there were those who escaped least marked, and being the most light-hearted, may be heard in our Palaces of Justice. The Glasgow advocate so believes in the power of the Word that he snatches the criminal from the very gate of the gallows. And there is statistical proof of his success, in that fewer persons are hung by the neck in Scotland than in England.

Finally, there is this great clamourous battalion who took to teaching, so convinced of the power of their words that they could take a child of five, vibrant, curious and alive, and, in ten tender years, so stun him that he could come out of school with less curiosity in his head than in his feet.

For remember, I don't talk of these smug and censorious fools who, like myself, stood at the despatch box anxious to say a coherent piece. They were the decorations, the Christians at the Roman holiday. I sing of the scores of unmuted and unsung Bridies who shot verbal arrows at these incidental figures throughout an entire evening. No-one got to his feet and sat down again—not even Togo—

without having his utterances subjected to the most scornful and detailed verbal scrutiny. The great art and wonder, the basis of abiding popularity was not so much the business of making speeches, but of composing a whole series of intensely personal and critical interruptions and hurling them at whatever audible target was performing. This sport made the Union and made the men of the Union : I gather from my occasional appearances there, that it still does.

At any rate, I want to believe that what was true of the Union in the Thirties or the Forties, will be as true in the Fifties and Sixties. Youth is not Youth unless it is brutal, at every business except one. It should always have a catapult in its hip pocket so that it may stone these old men who think to mount with wings as eagles. The ruthless young give the Union its reputation and its merit and there must be consolation in the fact that the Union has achieved something as characteristic, and perhaps as significant, as has been achieved by any of the Faculties. It would be greedy to ask more.

The Union too, must teach these golden lads and lasses the robust and elegant satisfaction that abides in the spoken and ephemeral word. I confess that because I cannot do otherwise I think that our day was ever better than those earlier swaggering years to which I refer. I still think it better to stutter about one proposition in which one passionately believes than to orate on a dozen, believing in none. But that aside, bark up some tree : the right one if possible, but up some tree. For this is the role of the Union.

THE STUDENT INTERNATIONAL CLUB.

By VICTOR S. GODFREY.

Victor S. Godfrey, an Indian Student who has lived for most of his life in South Africa, devotes part of his time to studying Dentistry and much of his energies to the furtherance of international goodwill. The Student International Club, of which Mr. Godfrey is a past President, has just celebrated its silver jubilee. This article tells of its aims and achievements.

In a Non-residential University like ours, one of the greatest handicaps for real University life is the lack of corporate life. It is true there are the two Unions, the Athletic and Political Clubs to give opportunity for those who desire something more than the classroom or laboratory work leading to a degree, but can one really say that there is any real corporate life in the University? It is bad enough for Scottish students, who though they may live a distance from the University and rush in for lectures and rush out in the evenings, at least, have their homes, Churches and Young People's Organisations to avail themselves of in their spare time. But how about the Students from Overseas? There are a great number of them in the University and almost 99% of them live in lodgings. Many a parent of these young students sends them to Britain, not only for the high standard of technical knowledge they can get here but more for them to acquire something of the culture and background of Britain and its great political and social life, instead of which they get only a poor and twisted view of British life in the picture houses and dance halls which is most of their extra-mural activity.

If one remembers that a very great proportion of these young people are the cream of the youth of their respective countries and that one day they will be returning to be leaders in every walk of life then the impressions they carry with them and the association they form and the cultural patterns they study will mean more both in their own lives and also in the wider sphere of international relationships than the technical knowledge and degrees they may acquire.

The Student International Club itself actually came into existence 25 years ago as an attempt to give practical realisation to an ideal expressed at the end of the First World War. This ideal, "to promote international under-standing by means of personal friendship among University students of many lands " is no less urgent and important at the present time than it was in 1918. Deeply convinced that the causes of war lie in international misunderstanding and lack of appreciation of one another's point of view and peculiar cultural, social and economic backgrounds, the young students of 25 years ago both Scottish and Overseas eagerly grasped the opportunity afforded by the presence of Students from all parts of the world in this great centre of learning, to build a new world of friendship and brotherhood. Glasgow University was thus among the first of British Universities to give tangible expression to the hopes and ideals of these students.

The Student International Club which is housed in its own premises at 11 University Gardens has thus been for 25 years a centre of friendship and fellowship for students from all parts of the world. During these years more than

6,000 students representing 56 different countries have come under the friendly influence of the club and have now gone back to positions of great responsibility. Perhaps one such instance will be timely—the Rt. Hon. Hector McNeil, the present Scottish Secretary, was one of the Club's members in his student days. In sending greetings to the club on it's twenty-first Birthday he wrote, "My first experiences of international affairs were gained in our old Club at 11 University Gardens, they were warm and rich days." The Overseas Students have gone back as the friends of Britain and of all the noblest things that Britain stands for, because they came to know Scottish homes and institutions through the friendship of Scottish Students.

The Club has always provided an atmosphere in which all points of view could be fearlessly expressed with the knowledge that there is a genuine desire among its members to understand and learn and to broaden their vision and deepen their sympathies.

While the club has these great ideals in the International sphere it has been mindful of the immediate personal needs of Students from abroad, one of the greatest being suitable lodgings. The club has always maintained a list of cheerful and comfortable homes to which students on arrival could be sent and where they will receive a warm welcome which soon dispels the initial sense of loneliness and homesickness in a strange city with its strange social background. An attempt is also made to meet these students at the docks and various stations on their arrival here, by Scottish students, which gives any Overseas Student a real feeling of welcome and confirms the fact that " Glasgow is a Friendly City."

A very interesting programme is arranged throughout the year to enable Overseas Students to come into the intellectual, social and spiritual fellowship first with their Scottish fellow students and then with students from other nations.   Each National Group in the Club is given an opportunity to share its unique culture, special gifts and peculiar problems and aspirations with other National Groups.

Opportunities are also afforded to Overseas Students to know something of the deeper life of Scotland as expressed in her homes, Churches and other institutions. Groups of Students from the Club are regularly invited throughout the year to homes and Young People's Socials.

It can be readily realised that too often, owing to habits of reserve or lack of thoughtfulness on the part of some Britishers as well as to lack of opportunity on the part of the British people these students from overseas sometimes return to their homes, embittered in spirit having seen only the less desirable and superficial elements of British life. This is where the Club with its high proportion of Scottish members renders the greatest possible service. During these 25 years of the Club's existence it has succesfully fought some of the silly prejudices and attitudes to Overseas students, so much so that the students of the present day could hardly believe there were ever such prejudices at all.

In this Silver Jubilee Year of the Club it is hoped that some of the finest and most influential of Scottish Students will join the Club and in fellowship with their Overseas fellow students make the next 25 years of the Club richer still in its very important task of building up brotherhood among men through friendship among University students.

THAE STUDENTS

How Charities Day brought Town and Gown together
By C. A. OAKLEY, B.Sc., Ed.B.

C.A. Oakley, the Ochre of G.U.M. Cartoons edited the first independent Ygorra in 1928 and has kept a fatherly eye on Charities Week ever since. A graduate of the Engineering Faculty Mr. Oakley forsook the precise sciences and is lecturer in industrial psychology. At the beginning of the War he was seconded to the Ministry of Aircraft Produc- as Scottish Controller and he now holds a similar position with the Board of Trade. He is at present engaged in writing a history of the Union and helping to edit a book of G.U.M. Cartoons.

THAE Students! For several hundred years the people of Glasgow have dismissed either with tolerant indifference or with tetchy irritation the latest bit of undergraduate light-hearted nonsense.

Perhaps, in days gone by, the fun of it all was by no means appreciated, for sometimes in the conflicts which took place occasionally between the town and gown the student got rough, and even did incidental destructive rioting.

There was, in fact, a good deal of trouble around about the 1820's during Thomas Campbell's various Rectorial elections; but afterwards over most of the Victorian era

I

the student was well held down by his mentors—the relationship between professor and undergraduate being that of the schoolmaster and pupil. Then a new tendency to indulge in larks showed itself in the noisy 'eighties and the gay 'nineties.

Possibly this indulgence in pranks reflected notions acquired from the new kind of school story, then being popularised by Talbot Baines Reed and which later came to radiant bloom in those penny weeklies, packed with diverting tales about ripping japes, the *Magnet* and the *Gem*.

This is demonstrated in the amusing story of the stolen Matric. Cards, before the John Bright Rectorial Address in March, 1883—a story which, by the way, was retold with illustrations in the *G.U.M.* of February, 1910. The Senate had allocated all of the best seats to prominent citizens, and had arranged for the students to stand at the back of the hall in what were described as " strongly constructed cattle pens." As numbers even for this privilege were limited, students wishing to be considered for tickets were invited to deposit their Matric. Cards in a box. These were to be returned to them later, with admission tickets for the lucky ones.

When all the Matric. Cards had been deposited according to instructions, someone stole the box. Next day Gilmorehill was in a turmoil, though there was an undercurrent of fearfulness. The Professor of Divinity told his class that the theft was " an outrage without parallel in human history, sacred or profane." As the Matric. Cards were missing, however, the Senate, " after sitting all day and so late into the night that supper had to be brought in," decided that the cattle pens should be removed and that anyone presenting himself who said he was a student would have to be admitted. " On the day after the Address the tickets, neatly arranged in alphabetical order, and addressed ' to a repentant Senate ' were found by the Principal's cook on the doorstep when she went to take in the milk."

Other sprees of this kind do not, however, hide the fact that the two most often recalled exploits of these decades were really turbulent disturbances, in which students came into conflict with police.

The first took place in 1896 outside the Ice Skating Palace, situated where the Regal Cinema now stands in Sauchiehall Street. It had no deeper cause than the refusal of admission to groups of students coming away from a Rectorial torchlight procession. The management ill-advisedly turned a fire hose on the students, and the trouble that followed landed eight of the participants in the cooler. The charges against them were subsequently found "not proven," but the citizens had not forgotten the incident when another took place.

This was in 1909. A mountebank who called himself Dr. Walford Bodie was appearing at the Coliseum, the city's largest music-hall. He had spoken sneeringly about the medical profession and the large body of students who attended one of the performances to express their displeasure found themselves involved in a " battle-royal " with the police. This time five appeared before the Bailie, who fined one, admonished one, and dismissed the other three.

The First Charities Days.

In 1919, after the First World War, the most rumbustious generation in the University's history appeared at Gilmorehill, and fears were felt that some frightful incident might occur between perhaps a party of exuberant ex-service students and certain townspeople who at that time were not of a particularly pacific turn of mind. Nor was the concern ill-founded, as those who took part in a procession to and from the Princess's Theatre on the occasion of a theatre night in February, 1920, will recall.

No one was more worried about all this than the University authorities who had the founding of the Student Welfare Fund in the back of their minds, and accordingly wanted town and gown to be on good terms.

An idea which our sister University at Aberdeen had conceived for dealing with an identical problem in the Granite City was seized upon. It was, in effect, holding a fancy dress parade during which a collection would be taken for the hospitals. The irrepressible high spirits were thus to be worked off in a way likely to gain public acclaim. So, in 1921, Infirmaries Day, or Students' Day, later to be Charities' Day, and still later Charities' Week, came into being.

When I was asked to write the history of this venture— which has, by now, raised well over £250,000 for Glasgow's charities—I turned up my set of *Ygorra Magazines*. They incidentally brought back to me a struggle during the middle 'twenties over the form the *Ygorra* should take. The first numbers contained in the main reproductions of articles and poems from the *G.U.M.* But then Manchester University, our keenest competitor in raising the largest total each year, brought out its *Rag Mag,* a specially written job with scores of burlesqued advertisements. It made a profit that shook us. In 1928 the *Ygorra* was at last handed over by the *G.U.M.* editorial committee to the Charities Day Committee, and for several years afterwards reached a standard which unfortunately it has not maintained.

I mention these *Ygorras*, however, because I found something among the tattered pages of that 1928 *Ygorra* that I had forgotten. It seemed that I had written up the history of Charities Day for that number. And, as my memory of what happened in those early days was a good

deal fresher 22 years ago than it is now, I shall do some
" lifting" from what I wrote then.

" That distant morning of 1921 when the first foray
stole from Gilmorehill and descended upon a city,
unsuspecting, undreaming of the intensity to which the
Charities Day collecting would develop and the ultimate
enormity of the ransom, seems of the very long ago.
Few of the enthusiasts of the first Day are now left at
the University, once more to rattle their boxes in the
faces of a Glasgow public unfailingly generous. Others,
energetic and enthusiastic as their predecessors, have
come to take their places, but Charities Day is grown
from a mere possibility to an established institution in
the civic calendar.

" In the beginning the hope was to collect £1,000.
Instead, the collection totalled £4,000. Yet it is not the
scene of enthusiasm which took place in the Union when
this total was announced which is the best remembered
incident of the first Charities Day. The place is reserved
for the first *Ygorra Special,* for, whilst the Weather
Clerk treated the Day itself with consideration, he did
not extend the same sympathetic treatment to the *Ygorra
Special.* When it went on sale in the streets, it snowed,
and snowed, and snowed ! Yet the magazine was sold out.

" On the whole, we cannot grumble at the way in
which the Weather Clerk has treated us. One fit of
choler on his part and many thousands are lost to the
hospitals. On only one Charities Day have we had
really bad weather, that of 1924, when snow and sleet
cleared the streets at luncheon time; and if the days of
1925 and 1926 were somewhat damp we can forgive
everything when we remember those of 1923 and 1927.

" We are always being asked why we hold Charities
Day in January—why not in May or June, when there is
a popular presumption of warmer weather? The

answer is simple. Some of the Faculties, such as Engineering, close their session in March. We are forced, willy-nilly, to choose one of the winter months, and we pick January, not for any love for the month, but simply because it is one pleasantly free from examinations; one which allows us to build up the organisation during the Christmas holidays."

By and large, what was written after eight Charities Days about Glasgow's weather has remained true. We had chanced upon a good weather spell in mid-January. There have been, so far as I can recall, only two Charities Days on which the conditions have been dreadful. On the majority of the others no rain has fallen, and during almost a dozen the sun has shone all day.

The 'Twenties.

A review of Charities Days falls easily into three periods, the 'twenties, the 'thirties, and the late 'forties. During the first two Charities Days the procession and the street side shows in the afternoon were what mattered. The set pieces, the decorated lorries and the costumes were much more elaborate than afterwards.

The craving to rival the Carnival of Nice was abandoned for the third Charities Day. Collecting became the thing, and an effort was made to get the collectors to go to the districts in the afternoon, to gather half-crowns by house-to-house visitations instead of ha'pennies in Sauchiehall Street. In 1926 the drive to boost the total began, and during the next few years had an astonishing triumph. Today it is perhaps best remembered because of some of the publicity devices used—particularly, of course, Miss Anne d'Apenny's trans-Atlantic swim, a hoax which took no fewer than 40,000 spectators to the Broomielaw to see the muscular young woman at the conclusion of her phenomenal performance. The slogan itself, And a Penny, was one of the most brilliant ever thought of for a charity campaign; but, although it was quite effective for Students' Day, it would probably have been better applied to some other scheme on a national scale, which allowed shop assistants to point to a collection box beside their cash registers and say to their customers as they picked up their change " and a penny!" The idea had been thought out by a Lancastrian, Bill Jones, and looking back on it I feel we rather wasted it.

A good deal of the success of these years was not, however, attributable to these publicity artifices. The replanning of house-to-house collections came into it too. So did the new *Ygorra*—which one year made a *profit* of £3,000—and the introduction of theatrical cabaret nights at the dance halls. Charities Day, in fact, expanded into Charities Week, although all collecting was still restricted to the Saturday.

In 1929 Glasgow was hit by an influenza epidemic and in consequence there were 2,000 fewer collectors than usual. The total actually gathered was £16,000, but such was the town's keenness for the students to go on " beating the record " each year, that Sir John Cargill gave £1,000 to the fund on the Monday, so that the advance would not be checked.

The totals distributed during the 'twenties and the slogans used, after their introduction in 1926, were :

1921	....	£4,000.
1922	....	£4,600.
1923	....	£7,000.
1924	....	£5,600.
1925	....	£7,400.
1926 (£10,000 this time or bust in the attempt)	....	£10,600.
1927 (And a Penny)	....	£14,700.
1928 (Add a Penny)	....	£16,500.
1929 (More!)	....	£17,000.

The 'Thirties.

That year, 1929, was the last in which men who had been closely associated with Charities Day from its beginning took an active part. A change in outlook was conveyed to the people of Glasgow by the " new hands " on the first page of the 1930 *Ygorra*. " We must dispel the impression that has got abroad that this Day is to be a less elaborate affair than past Days. The only important changes are that there will be no Cabarets and no dolls. The Cabarets were not, financially, worth the enormous amount of labour expended in their organisation. Neither were the dolls, which brought in a very small profit on a large turnover. . . . Can we keep it up? Of course, we cannot hope that the collection will go on increasing every year. We expect to find the total stabilising itself round a certain figure. What the figure will be, who knows? " I wonder what Sir John Cargill thought when he read that?

Yet the men who wrote it *did* break the record. They were helped by the impetus of the organisation that had been already built up, the addition of 2,000 collectors over the previous year, a wonderfully sunny day, and a chance that brought the Rector, Mr. Stanley Baldwin, to Glasgow to take the march past with the Lord Provost. But see from the totals quoted below what happened afterwards. " A stabilised total, forsooth!"

Even more astonishing, at least to their predecessors, was what was written on the first page of the 1931 *Ygorra*. "The truth is, in spite of our optimistic slogan, Up! we do not expect to break another record. We intend to do our best. On this occasion, however, Charities Day will not be advertised to be bigger and better than ever, but to be as good as ever." Well, they were not embarrassed by breaking the record. They brought the total down to almost £3,000 below the previous year's. As one Glasgow newspaper observed, the policy had seemed to be down! not up!

It is, indeed, difficult for one who took part in organising Charities Day in the 'twenties to keep his patience when writing some of the things done in the years that followed. One bright convener of immunity badges started raffling them in smoke rooms and could not understand why the business men who used to pay a pound for a badge each year stopped doing so. Another, as the year's stunt, pretended to run a Dublin Sweep and instead got himself involved in a futile and apparently endless argument with Church Leaders. The old principle of having no shows arranged for the Friday evening before Charities Day, so that collectors could start fresh and not wilt the next day, was shelved and a midnight film show was arranged for the Paramount Cinema.

Slogans were adopted which seemed to be nothing more than pointless playing with names. Worst of all S.R.C. discussions on whether the Day should be scrapped altogether—on the ground that it took students away from their books—were reported in the public press. The fact that it is often easier to get bad publicity than good publicity had to be learned the hard way. Here are the totals for the thirties :

1930	(Somoa)	£17,750.
1931	(Up!)	£15,000.
1932	(Up Doublin!)	£11,500.
1933	(Can It!)	£11,600.
1934	(Canarder)	£11,900.
1935	(Come Clean)	£9,000.
1936	(Addus Abbawbee)	£9,050.
1937	(Fill-it-O)	£9,000.
1938	(Wreck that Record!)	£10,900.
1939	(Canmore)	£8,100.
1940	(*Only Charities Day during War*)	£6,900.

The 'Forties.

In 1946, the announcement that Charities Day was to be resumed brought joy to some old stagers, but even they were startled to read that the goal was £25,000. Strange stories have since been told about how this figure was arrived at. Whatever the truth may be, the essential point is that this time the record was well and truly wrecked. Philip McCan raising £23,200 in 1946, and Uno Ygorra £26,000 in 1947. The totals have continued to be excellent.

I know nothing about how this has been achieved. I have been told that a list of the ranks held in the Fighting Services by some of the men who got Charities Day going again in 1946 makes impressive reading. Perhaps, however, what mattered most was not the skill these experienced men applied to the organisation of the Day, but the gusto with which they did it. And the originality too, for certainly no Charities Days in the past produced so many fresh ideas.

A recent tendency for the totals to fall slightly instead of to rise is, however, a little disturbing, and raises the question of how good these recent achievements really are? Those who ran Charities Day in the late 'twenties estimated Glasgow's capacity as £25,000. But the pound is worth a good deal less now than then. Also there is a reminder in the allocation after 1922 of one-quarter of the money collected to the Lord Provost's Unemployment Fund, that Glasgow was not a particularly prosperous city in the two decades between the Wars. Glasgow folk had a lot more cash in their pockets in the 'forties than they had in the 'twenties and 'thirties. Perhaps, therefore, Glasgow's limit should be put nowadays at £35,000 rather than at £25,000.

If, in conclusion, a suggestion or two were asked from someone who has had nothing to do with running Charities Day since 1929, and probably doesn't know what he is talking about anyhow, I would comment that it is perhaps

a mistake to have a lot of pre-Charities Day publicity
stunts.   One, put over big, is more effective than a score,
no matter how good, that get in each other's way.   Girl
students descending on senior business men in their offices
can raise as much as £5,000 by selling them Immunity
Badges—or, as they should be called, Immunity Shields,
for a dim-wit in the past failed to grasp the significance
of the shield as a protection against collectors, and his
mistake in using the word badge has gone on for a long
time now.   And, finally, the dolls, or something else
to interest children, should be re-introduced.   Beauty
queens delight the eyes of readers of the picture press, but
they have plenty of other things to interest them.   It is
the children who look forward to Charities Day each year
and they are worth cultivating.

THE UNION
By W. G. A. CRAIG, President of the Union.

*A former pupil of Glasgow High School W. G. A.
Craig matriculated in the Faculty of Arts in 1942 and
completed only one year before going to the Navy.
He served in the Navy from 1943 to 1947 and rose
to the rank of Able Seaman. On returning to polite
life he took an active part in National politics and is
on the Scottish Committee of the Liberal Party. He
was Convener of Debates in 1948/9, Secretary of the
the Union 1949/50 and is President of the Union in
the Fifth Centenary Year. Who better than he can
commit that intangible something which is the Union
to paper ?*

Once a year a portrait of the Union is attempted in that
feast of propaganda and polemic—the Student's Handbook, and like most recurrent traditions the portrait has
developed a certain classical simplicity and authority of
form. The reader is introduced in some fanciful manner
to the billiard room on the top floor of the building and
thence gently guided through the material resources of
No. 32 University Avenue, to the alliteration of boilers,
baths, and barber in the basement.

This geographical approach to the problem, while it
may be of some use to the incoming "Fresher" seems to
me to escape rather than to achieve the description of

THE UNION

the Union. The reality of the institution as distinct from its abode might more readily be outlined by the historical method—indeed the prevalent heresy that the Union is the large building at the University Tram Terminus would be laid by the realisation that the Union's present home is a recent acquisition, no older than the Certificates of Fitness of our more experienced undergraduates. The building which earlier generations happily remember is that cosier if smaller place up the hill, which, after the manner of Eve's production from a part of the original Adam, became on our departure, The Queen Margaret Union, to Adam's eternal delight. Be that as it may, the history of the Union is being dealt with in another place by an abler pen than mine.

"When in doubt what to say quote a few statistics" has been the salvation of many a contemporary politician, and I have no doubt that there are those who would be interested to learn that the Union has 2,000 (or is it 3,000) members in addition to a vast army of Life Members scattered all over the globe, that it has two boilers, six baths, eight billiard tables, thirteen fireplaces, and that its annual cake production is numbered in hundreds of thousands—indeed we understand that the Union is the only Catering Establishment (for we are a Catering Establishment according to the Ministry of Food) in Glasgow to send representatives to the recent National Catering Exhibition in London. A more interesting and probably more illuminating departure would perhaps be a graphical correlation of the incidence of "breaking and entering" dances, with the discipline meted out by the Board of Management at its periodical meetings—more illuminating, because it demonstrates some of the importance of the Union to the student body.

If we are to find a "social purpose" for the Union, and in these days not to have a social purpose is to be

" anti-social," we would rather ignore the mundane feed-ings of students—necessary as that may be—and argue that the value of the Union lies in this factor of self-discipline; the Union receives its members from the irresponsible and authoritarion environment of the school and introduces them to a society in which, for better or for worse, they are responsible and the only authority is that of the community of which they are part; the essence of the institution is that it is governed, not merely administered, by the students themselves—the direct connection between error and personal disadvantage is very clear; there is full opportunity for mistakes to be made, but there is no shield from their consequences. In addition to this negative but necessary lesson in responsibility there is a considerable field of action in which the student body, and the individual student, can practice the arts of living in community, of exercising justice, of preferring efficiency to humanity, or vice versa, of weigh-ing alternative uses of corporate resources, as he has not had the opportunity before. This experience of what might be called the " pilot scheme " of adult society, provided by the Union, is certainly an important argument in favour of its retention in the Welfare State, an adequate justification of the enlightened policy of some Local Education Authorities who provide grants for subscriptions to what they are pleased to call " University Clubs "; yet the value of the Union to some of its members, its potential value to all, is not merely this education in social administration but an introduction to a much older, more fundamental benefit of society.

Man is not a gregarious animal because of the possibility of social insurance or the economies of a communal water-supply, but simply because he loves the companionship of his fellow-men; the mutual fertilisation of differing minds, the infinite variety of group activity; the incomparable satisfaction of joint endeavour—all these are denied the solitary individual or the solitary student whose society is the limited one of those pursuing his own specialisation, whose endeavour is confined to the narrow field of private attainment.

The University has recently been described as a "Conversation"; in its heyday it was a self-conscious organism—to-day it is tending, like knowledge itself, to an introspective departmentalism where conversation, if not forbidden, finds little to encourage it. In this disintegrating society the Union provides one of the few forces of cohesion cutting across specialisations, and the most effective catalyst is enjoyment. The classical student song, dating from a time when men and not buildings made a University, " Gaudeamus igitur, dum juvenes sumus," might in our own time return the chill echo " Enjoy yourself, it's later than you think," for in enjoying himself in his own way the student of to-day is practising a dying art. The incredible diversity of enjoyments found in the Union, ranging from the activities of the group formed to sing madrigals to those of the crusaders for World Government is an oasis in the contemporary desert of organised entertainment, as passive and synthetic as pleasure. In this and above all in Union Debates, are flat men made round and narrow men broad; in learning and teaching the art of enjoyment, the Union member, being both teacher and student learns something perhaps as valuable as the technique of splitting atoms, equating supply and demand, or prolonging life beyond the Biblical three score years and ten.

In setting itself up as a self-confessed school of enjoyment, in an age in which utility, social purpose and the virtue of austerity are the " trinodas necessitas," the Union may appear as an anachronism. It is none the worse for that.

THE STUDENT IN PRINT
By I. P. C. MURRAY.

The author of this article was educated at Loretto and Matriculated in the Faculty of Medicine in 1947. In 1948 he served his apprenticeship on the staff of the G.U.M. and the following year he edited the Student's Handbook. He was raised to the Editorship of the G.U.M. in 1950 and holds the position for the Fifth Centenary Year.

" Intended as an antidote against the prevailing errors of the present day."

Such is the Editor's aim as presented on the title page of " *The Glasgow Universalist's Miscellany* " or "The Medium for Impartial Discussion," one of the earliest of several student publications which appeared in the first half of the last century.

The Universalist, a drab leatherbound volume of 550 pages first appeared in 1813 and, by present standards, was heavy not only in appearance. A glance down the imposing list of contents shows headings such as " Proof of the Existence of Fallen Angels," "An Instance of Papal Intolerance " and the proceedings of many Missionary Society Meetings. An apparent anomaly is headed " A recent case in the Infirmary of Glasgow." On examination however, there is nothing medical about the case as it turns out to be a five page treatise on " Death, Fear and Faith."

Even a topical " Ode to Bonaparte " proves to be theological in character, starting :

> *" May peace, Sieur Napoleon, attend thy retreat,*
> *Religion console thee, instead of the great,*
> *The Saviour of mankind thy guardian still be*
> *While they his example copied in thee."*

The first regular periodical of the century was *The Student* which produced twenty-two issues every Saturday in 1817, filled with poems in English, Latin and Greek. There was nothing more until 1826 when the *Philosophical Tatler* and *The Academic* appeared. The latter was a fortnightly twelve page paper and, like the *Tatler*, only lasted a few months. It was, however, revived the following year as *The Collegian* and contained more news, several excellent etchings and the first debate reports. In its seven fortnightly issues, more than two thirds was occupied by essays continued in serial form from number to number. Such serials were " On Epic and Dramatic Poetry " (in three parts) and " The difference between Wit and Humour" (in two parts). 1828 saw the brief life of *Alma Mater* of which it is recorded that one of the early subscribers was Mrs. Bogle of Gilmorehill.

Another literary magazine of short duration was *The Athenaeum* which was published in 1830. It would appear to be the first to invite outside contributions but this did not stay its fate.

This somewhat didactic style invaded most of the student publications of the time. *The College Album,* a large tome similar to the *Universalist,* appeared from 1828 to 1874, at first every two years, but later more irregularly. The heavy manner of its contents makes it hard to believe that it was truly representative of the undergraduates of this period. The 1832 Cholera Epidemic, however, called forth a lighter poem by a leading member of the University Temperance Society.

K

> " *The man who keeps his stomach pure,*
> *And tipples not at whisky toddy*
> *In spite of cholera, walks secure*
> *No spasms rack his body.*"

It became *The Glasgow University Album* in 1840 and, among the very prosaic contents, are previously unpublished letters by Walter Scott and the Rectorial Address of Lord MacAulay. The only space devoted to the Fourth Centenary in the 1851 Album is a very short note on famous Glasgow graduates, this volume, like several others, being dedicated to Queen Victoria.

It was not until 1846 that the Student Press threw off these rather oppressive reins and produced papers more characteristic of traditional student humour. That year saw the birth of three publications—*College Squib, Glasgow Punch,* and *The Literary Magazine*—and also watched them fade into oblivion.

Squib, starting with an announcement in the first editorial that they were determined to have " fearless exposure of crammed dunces whose efforts to carry away class honours are but too often crowned with success," was a fortnightly four page paper, costing twopence, and had a triumphant, if short-lasting, life. The editors claimed that " on the sensational days of publication, Hadden's shop was beseiged for hours." Rivalry was intense between *Squib* and *Punch,* which had appeared first although production had started after the launching of its competitor.

Much of the first edition of *Squib* is taken up with a vigorous attack on *Punch.* " We were led to believe that it was to be an attempt at wit of some sort. There is, however, but one joke in the first number and, as that one serves to prove that there ought not to have been any, the circumstance is to be regretted."

The first two issues were successful beyond the editor's

hopes—the second requiring three editions to satisfy the demand to read about "The Great College Riots." These resulted after a gate had been built across a lane commonly used by students as a short cut to the Old College in "their desire for punctuality." One morning, therefore, thirty red gowned students proceeded to demolish the offending obstacle—" the only enemy being a very ferocious specimen of the softer sex who attempted to stay progress by discharging on them copious buckets of infamously dirty water." The crowd of students grew and the work of destruction continued apace until the arrival of the police. The sequel was the appearance of several students before the magistrates, with three on the bench instead of the usual one. A great array of counsels, however, procured an acquittal, much to the general delight, and it was noted gratefully that " the prisoners were treated with all courtesy due to their distinguished rank."

The third and fourth editions just paid their way, the latter dealing at length with " Baths and cheap Shaving for Medical Students." Among many reprisals in *Punch,* one poem forecast *Squib's* fate (perhaps also slightly topical to-day?)

They'll carry me away from my studies so poetical,
I fear everyday to the Militia I'll get a call
And then, woe's me, what will become without me, O
Of the gallant College Squib *that frightens* Punch *so*
strongly, O."

This proved to be too true as, after the fourth number, the editor "became fevered" and the *Squib was* extinguished.

It had, however, outlived *Punch* by thirteen days as the latter also only lasted four issues. Starting as the organ of the University Conservative Party, it soon broke away from the whip. Edited by four students, none of whom, it is recorded, ever obtained a degree, *Glasgow Punch* was a fortnightly eight paged publication, most of whose contents, like its rival, were " written by Mathematics and Latin classes in a hurry and often extremely personal and vulgar." The first issue resulted in Lang's in St. Vincent Street being completely blocked until more copies arrived. After this, apparently, sales fell off and it died a financial death.

Both *Squib* and *Punch* turned without mercy on *The Literary Magazine* calling it " a heterogeneous mass of puns, steam, love, asterisks, and theology." The editors, who had dared to call themselves " a very promising set of young men," were reviled on all sides as " a most distressing set of young snobs," and the organ of the Literary Debating Society went the way of its contemporaries.

It seems that there were few publications, apart from *College Album,* for many years after this. An attempt in 1868 with *College Miscellany* failed because the students had no longer any desire for the sombre style of writing.

There have been, however, many odd papers and magazines published at intervals, especially in the last fifty years, all serving some definite purpose rather than being solely for entertainment. Several departmental publications appeared, especially for Divinity and Engineering, but the medical student has been best served. After a short-lived *College Stethoscope, The Scalpel* was published in 1836 but became unpopular with the authorities as " Its gross attacks on personalities are inconsistant with University decorum." It finally became so outrageous that it was suppressed with great firmness. The present medical journal *Surgo,* has built up a fine reputation inside and outside Glasgow in recent years.

Political clubs have occasionally raised enough money to launch an abortive magazine, the most recent being *Conflict* and *Tinker's Cuss.* The first to appear was the *Peel Club Papers,* the organ of the forerunner of the

Conservative Club, and was mainly filled with vigorous attacks on the alleged shortcomings of the Liberals. Rectorial elections have also always brought forth a spate of short-lived pamphlets—*The College Unionist, Gorst Elector* and others—not forgetting, of course, *The Blue Bunnet,* the most prominent in the great pamphlet campaign of the recent Rectorial. The great series of *Ygorras* introduced in the twenties in association with Charities Week, deserves mention as much of the best writing and drawing by students is to be found therein.

It was only in 1889, after the move to Gilmorehill, that a regular University Magazine, written by students for the entertainment of students, was produced. A *Glasgow University Magazine* had appeared in 1882, becoming the *Glasgow University Review* in the following year.

Six years passed, however, before the publication of the *G.U.M.* started the regular record run which remains unbroken to-day despite ups and downs in standard and publishing difficulties of three wars.

Two years ago it celebrated its Diamond Jubilee and generations of undergraduates have recognised it as an established feature of University life. It is still held in such high regard by the older generations that many deplore the modern tendency to compress its initials into one sticky word!

The first editor, according to the records, A. S. Blacklock, was a brilliant student, particularly distinguished in English literature, and the firm foundations laid by him have stood the test of time. In the early Magazines, there are contributions from James Bone, John Buchan, Gilbert Murray and J. J. Bell (Wee Magreegor) who was editor in 1896. A long list of editors, many of them well known in the outside world, lies behind us now. Each provided his piece in the building up of the tradition of the *G.U.M.* There was the great series of the Edwardians—the

Brownings, A. S. Wallace, George Fletcher, O. H. Mavor, and Walter Elliot. The line continues with Foster Franklin, John Burt, Gilbert Highet, Robert Murray, Allan MacKinnon, and more recently, Lindsay Kerr, and Bingo Mavor. The great artists of the magazine—C. A. Oakley, Ian Phillips, and Hugh Johnstone—have also left their mark and their drawings are still being used.

The only rival to the *G.U.M.* came with the appearance of *The Gilmorehill Globe* in the autumn of 1932. This was a weekly newspaper, price one penny, " to cater for a special side of University life—the voracious gossip-hungry, light conversational side, leaving the *G.U.M.* to provide the more serious cultural entertainment." It met with great success until it faded in 1935. Its triumph lay in the fact that in addition to reporting up-to-date news (impossible in a magazine),it dared to criticise whom and what it pleased. This brought fresh life into the student world but the editors were, at all times, very careful not to overstep the mark and attack anything that might have repercussions outside their own world.

It was the failure to keep within this margin with regard to alleged " Charities Week Scandals " that led to the downfall of *The Gilmorehill Girn,* a similar paper which ran for several issues in 1949-1950. The scathing attacks on many prominent student officials produced surprising and often satisfactory results. The demand for each issue must have rivalled that of the *Squib* a hundred years previously. The final compulsory closure was seen with regret by many, but most of them realised the folly of the editor's indiscretions.

With the *Girn, The Gilmorehill Guardian* died also. A remarkable individual effort, it attempted to remain unbiased—and thereby cut its own financial throat. The failure of these two leaves Glasgow once again as the only

Scottish University without a newspaper, but we hope that this may soon be remedied.

Such is a brief history of the Student Press of our University. It shows that there has been, during at least the last century and a half, a real demand for such publications. But what of its future?

To-day a strongly competitive National Press presents a constant challenge and it is essential that the Student Press, if it is to survive strong and alert, maintaining its fine traditions, must be individual and must not ape others.

It should set itself up to be an integral part of the social life of the University, moulding itself to the characteristics of that life, and prove thereby that it is as esential to the general well-being of its own world as the national press is to the world outside.

It is interesting to note that since 1814, there have been continuous attempts to reform " the prevailing errors of the present day," the efforts meeting with varied success—perhaps all students are " *Girners* " at heart! The suggestion has been made that the University newspapers and magazines are now merely nurseries for primary training of budding journalists. This may be true of the older English Universities, but it certainly does not apply to ours, as can be seen in the fact that four of the seven most recent editors of the *G.U.M.* have been students of medicine.

The Student Press has, therefore, an essential part to play in integrating and recording all the aspects of the undergraduate life of a University, as seen in this Commemoration Volume. It ought not to step outside this world, as it is most desirable that it should reflect the character of the student of each generation to the future undergraduate in the same way that, from to-day, we can look back to 1814.

THE REGISTRAR

By John S. Young.

John S. Young matriculated at Glasgow University in the year of the Ninth Jubilee. Since graduating he has been a Factory Inspector and has served in the Censorship Service. His passion for getting to know things found ample scope in these occupations and in this article he tells of his apprenticeship to the masters of learning.

In July 1950, after more than forty years' absence from the Quadrangle, I found a notice on the wall, from the Editor of the Commemoration Volume. It read:—" Write to me what you please; you may get Five Pounds."

This notice excited me; but not nearly so much as some notices which a few decades earlier I had scanned (in vain) on the same wall.

" Ignorance," wrote Shakespeare, " is the primal curse." It may be; but provided it is complete and its possessor knows not of it—'tis a blissful though perhaps a deplorable state of being.

Knowledge, even the scantiest, is an unsettling thing. At twenty-three years of age my ignorance was profound. However, be not deceived. It was not complete. I knew a thing or two. Yes. In the Calico Print Works by the river Glasert, a tributary of the Kelvin, I had learned many things and had found time to read many heaps of volumes. Deadwood Dick and Dick Turpin, Four-Revolver Pete, and other heroic figures were well known to me.

I can still remember the pang of regret when, at fifteen years of age, I made the melancholy discovery that it was the same story, with different names, that I was reading. Four-revolver Pete, or Hugh, no longer interested me. What was now to be done?

The only book in the village was " The Pilgrim's Progress." That production—apart from the Greek Dramatists, Virgil, Dante and Milton (his prose excepted) —is the most unreadable book that ever was. En passant, they call these writers the "Ancients." What a misnomer! *We* are the Ancients. Those fellows were the Primitives —the Barbari, as Caesar called the scantily clad hordes who gathered on our southern cliffs, with their buggies, to frighten him, if they could . . . The new Caesars now call us Bourgeois, Cosmopolitan, Opportunist, tame epithets indeed, in appearance, but loaded with much more scornful if not terrifying connotation.

I can, as allowed by the foregoing notice, write as I please : but to come back to the point. My ignorance was becoming pitifully apparent, a fatal thing, to me.

I asked our cobbler, at the corner of Balmano Brae and Rottenrow, "How does one get rid of ignorance? " " Where and how does one get to know things?"

Clap an extinguisher on your irony when dealing with a Scot, is one of the rare " howlers " of Charles Lamb. He, probably, had met only one—Thomas Carlyle, who preferred direct and unmistakable forms of expression. " Forty millions, mostly fools." Carlyle uses too many words. He excites irony : is not exponent of it. From his " Silence in Fifty Volumes " that brief utterance is one " crack " worth quoting.

Well, the cobbler, with characteristic Scots irony, told

me that he believed that Gilmorehill was the place for a
difficult job of that sort. Ignoring the irony, on the following Monday morning, to Gilmorehill I went. I found the
Registrar and informed him that I wished to take the
classes at the University.

He looked at me : asked for my papers. " You have
with you, no doubt, your Higher School or Preliminary
Certificate."

I looked at him. Gabbling that I would come again
later I beat a confused retreat. I " advanced northwards."
A Russian General, round this date, had so reported when
the Japanese were chasing him from the south.

I had left the village school twelve years before this
date, on " finishing my education " and had not heard
of such things as " Preliminaries."

I soon found out. Before I could get rid of ignorance
or enter Gilmorehill, I had to pass an examination in Latin,
Mathematics, English and French . . . Latin? Who could
ever read that gibberish? Euclid? These absurd proposi-
tions—so obvious, until they asked you to prove them.
English? I had been using it for twenty years. French?
The French wrote, I had been told, only of one subject.
They discussed, I discovered, cursorily, of course, quite a
variety of subjects . . . But, I had to pass that " Preliminary," or remain in transparent ignorance for ever. After
thirty months of hard labour, in conjunction with that of
making a living, pass it I did, and satisfied that awe-
inspiring Registrar.

Ever since I have been " sitting and standing examinations," formal and informal. I have looked in all the books
they have written in half-a-score of jargons in the last two
thousand years, and more . . .

Did I reach my goal? Get rid of ignorance? Nay, verily.
On the contrary, my ignorance (and that of the scribes)
became more and more glaring. Was the effort worth

while? Yea, verily. To become aware of one's ignorance (and that of the scribes—Primitive or Ancient) is the most exhilarating, health-giving and amusing of all sports.

To get rid of the whole load of our ignorance might or might not be gay ; but it is not possible. Were our ration a thousand years instead of three score and ten, life would still be as the old Greek said, too short.

I wish the Registrar had been aware of the mass of ignorance before him on that morning. If he had, his loud laughter would still be echoing round the Quadrangle pillars.

THE CLYDESIDE AND THE DOCUMENTARY FILM
By JOHN GRIERSON, M.A., LL.D.

At various times University graduates have become tinkers, tailors, beggars and thieves. A few have even become rich men. John Grierson has made his name as none of these but as the originator of documentary films. His film " Drifters," produced in 1929, *is already a classic. Mr. Grierson is now Films Controller of the Central Office of Information. In this controversial article he tells of his aims in the world of films and indirectly of the effect the " Red " Clydeside has had on the University.*

When Universities celebrate their longevity the theme should, in propriety, have the weight of the occasion. It is pleasant to have the documentary film ride, or row, in the ceremonial galley, but I choose to think that it is merely because it signifies what various and strange conclusions may derive from academic premises and that it is this two-and-two-make-five of the University life which is its whole importance. I did not learn how to make movies at the University. My only film excursion at the time was a piece, which has since, in the light of events, come to be a minor critical curiosity, in the G.U.M., one of the earliest appreciations of C. Chaplain as the artist he is now allowed to be. But that is not important. What is, is the sense, more and more articulate as time goes on, of how the traditions of one's University affect whatever work a man may do.

I belonged to a generation of changes and changelings, though for that matter it was innocence itself to the laocoon twisting and turnings of our later moment. We were out of the first war and I suppose toughened by it as our present successors must be. But there was a difference and I think a precious difference. Our war was not so long that we had begun to take it seriously and, victim of the universal lack of education in world events, we did not know even the very little about its bearing which the present generation manifests—one hopes, manifests—about the last one. I will not say that we actually believed it was the war to end all wars but, in considerable gaiety of spirit, we acted as if it were. We accordingly took to peace with some certainty, a measure of excitement and even a degree of violence; and vis-à-vis the professors and their schools I can only remember that we were an ungentle people. We were going to change a lot of things.

On figures, we did not make a very evident revolution, but what did establish itself, and I think it was new, was that the University progressively came to see the shipyards from the hill and put more on the academic conscience, and in many spheres, than had been there before. Even the great Sir William Macewen took to what, at the time, seemed a pretty muddled brand of political consciousness, which he called the Middle Classes Union. We were not to know it, but it was to have more influence on the party of Mr. Attlee and Mr. Morrison than Marx, Kropotkin, Keir Hardie, Wheatley and John McLean combined. In fact, looking back on it, the pundits were as restless as their juniors. Sir Henry Jones was not getting the old theatrical reaction to " first the blade, then the ear, then the full corn "; and it was now possible to write philosophic songs that allowed quite dirty things to be done to the

Absolute. Latta was gently uncertain whether there could be any logical conclusion to anything any more, and no wonder; for Lord Lindsay of Birker was now filling in between melodramas and addressing mobs at the Metropole. Leonard Russell was pursuing the pluralistic universe with a single-mindedness that had begun to disturb him; and John Swinnerton Phillimore was passing in our Calvinist midst, and despite our notable influence, to the authority of the Catholic Church. Saurat was talking Taine and social significance, while MacNeile Dixon was doing his gracious best against such oncoming sansculottes as James Joyce, T. S. Eliot and D. H. Lawrence. Only one, R. Muir, stuck *sans vergogne* to the established classical certainties of his sarcomas, as they struck in the mines and rioted in George Square and marched the army against the local proletariat and ran political convicts for the Lord Rectorship. In and out and round about the academic legs jinked the men of the Clydeside, preparing, though they were later distressed to know it, the social democratic conquest of the Kingdom and the blessedness, presumably, of the meek. In one last Anarchic fling, not a few students tramped the streets giving what was probably the final airing in these Islands to the old war-cry "Abstain from Voting." If they did nothing else they at least brought forth the wrath of the great Lenin himself. " Left Wing Communism " he thundered from the East, " an infantile disorder."

This sensibility of the University to the events about it is the heart of one's memory of it and also the heart of one's debt to it. Glasgow in that sense has its own unique distinction. I cannot think of any University in which I have worked, not even Chicago, that Sears Roebuck catalogue of academic pursuit, where the realities of the town so penetrate the student life, or where the Faculties so affect each other. Perhaps we were lucky, but the

greatest teaching influence in Arts in my time came, not
from Arts, but from Medicine; and Kant to the surging
mind was not more significant than Kelvin. It somehow
made us all thundering little realists and relativists, no
matter what we took up. Indeed if you look at the people
who, like myself, took to the media, note over a generation
what a practical business we made out of it. It may be that
we started to be poets and prophets but the trouble was
that we were somehow under pressure to be engineers and
educators and social reformers and politicians and public
organisers and devoted graduates of Hawkhead as well.
In my own case, the succeeding formula was the documentary film. It was the best I could do to combine the several
duties which a richly disordered band of confused professors, dramatic and melodramatic medicine men and
itinerant rabble rousers had imposed upon me.

I do not mean by all this that the documentary film form
and its development across the world came especially from
the University influences of my time. There were of
course other forces afoot and elsewhere, all eager to seize
on the realistic capacities of this new mass medium of film
and use them for directive public purposes. Lenin, not
least, had already declared the film to be the most powerful
instrument of mass education in the hands of emergent
democracy and the one most to be encouraged by the Soviet
State; and we were to see the fruits of his policy in the
astonishing school of cinema which emerged in the middle
twenties around the great names of Eisenstein, Pudowkin,
Vertov and Dovshenko. Even as we sat in Glasgow in the
earlier twenties, Flaherty's *Nanook* was showing at the
Scala and sundry other peripatetic cameramen were at least
knocking out the back wall of the proscenium and exercising the medium's capacity for throwing open a window on
the world. Yet I have reason to make this point about
Glasgow and the mobilisation of the cinema for social

purposes. In no University of the time, I think, did the rich influences so combine as to suggest a venture which would do justice at once to the aesthetic, educational and social aspects of a problem. It was the continuing sense of this triple errand, certainly, which distinguished the character and development of the documentary film in Great Britain and made it subsequently the model for other countries to follow.

For me, the particular attractions of the cinema could then, as now, be set down quite sharply. It could get about, and was so tooled, by measure of varying lenses and varying speeds of perception, that it could well be a wonder-eye for the observation of a world which science and technology were lighting up on a thousand new perspectives. Even more important, the film's powers of composition made it possible to throw together in immediate proximity of space and time the apparently disparate, but related, images of a world, becoming, by reason of science and technology, even more complexly relative. Patently, the concept of the individual in space which had satisfied the painters and even the story tellers since the Renaissance was no longer satisfying either the painters or the story tellers. Likewise, even the concept of the person or individual as defined in the academies no longer satisfied actual experience : the experience, in particular, of a world in which Church, State, Community, Family and the patterns of order, justice and freedom which had been woven around them, were being forced to share their truth with new economic and organisational forces, the basic patterns of which had been only barely touched on by the arts and philosophies. In that sense, we saw, in the mass media, instruments for nothing less than the reconstitution of the civic imagination of our modern world.

What we said for film might well have been said for

other media; but it happened that it was for film that it was first and most strongly said. Here, we declared, is a medium which can be a powerful tool in the hands of emergent democracy. It can describe this new world which the new democracy is bound to inherit : and in the relative or co-operative terms which its political forms must inevitably follow. It can articulate the new order to come. It can bring alive to the masses, in a form and on a scale no other educational instrument can parallel, its possibilities, its privileges and its duties. So, with Leon Trotsky, we thought of art not as a mirror held up to nature, but as a hammer shaping it : though indeed, in our British way, we were more inclined to quote John Stuart Mill. We remembered that it was " Only in the hands of the artist that the truth becomes a living principle of action."

Without apology, I return the documentary idea thus to its origins, because the price of its astonishing success across the world has been the compromise of its first thoughts and principles. Any Glasgow man will follow me readily if I say that what largely happened to the documentary movement was what happened to the Clyde-side movement. It succeeded, or appeared to succeed, all too soon. We got what we wanted, or rather what, to many, we appeared to want; and, as though we had gone with our brethren to Parliament, we were in the fabian world of critical acceptance and appreciation before we had time to harden its radical core. There is perhaps nothing so embarrassing or, in the short run, so natively funny, as the British habit of turning telescopes to blind eyes and hailing warmly every incipient revolution in sight. When *The Times,* after all our pother on the Clyde, editorially welcomed Mr. Maxton to the counsels of the nation, it was of course not the beginning of an era, but the end of one that had hardly started. The development of the documentary film and its modification as the progressive creative force it was originally intended to be, were similarly assured when Mr. Elliot and his Conservative colleagues, with the everlasting *Times* not far behind, decided that this was the very thing for them and proceeded to make it their own.

Here I had better mention a moment in our parochial story which I have not before written about. In the late twenties this concept of mobilising the new media to positive and progressive ends was already very clear to me. I had spent some years mastering, or thinking to master, the first aesthetic problems involved. I had studied with Charles Merriam of Chicago not only the normal processes of mass information and their control but, more affectionately still, the problems and processes of propaganda : delving deviously into the unnatural ways of mass advertising, the yellow press and economic lobbies. Here, as I thought, was this great innocent the Cinema, unused, almost unobserved, yet the most powerful path of all to the imagination and the will. What more simple than to give the concept to the Labour movement and present to the progressive forces of the country a fast lead in using it to bring the working class, its destiny and all, in living terms to the screen? In my pattern of possibility, the Co-operative movement was to do what fell later to the hand of its competitor, Mr. Rank. I took the idea to Mr. Arthur Henderson; but if I have now to confess that nothing came of it, it is with the consolation that other, and it may be even better, ideas have gone to the Labour movement and have disappeared without trace. As I have indicated, Mr. Elliot, in one of Mr. Elliot's flashes of brilliant fielding, caught the idea in mid-air and presented it to his Conservative cohorts. They proceeded forthwith to bring the working class, its destiny and all, in living terms to the screen, without a single doubt or bother in the world. Even the oncoming surge of realist films from the Soviet Union was taken in their feudal stride. Certain members of the Conservative Cabinet turned themselves into what must have been the most exclusive private film society on record and were graduate students of Potemkin and the rest before the London Film Society had struggled loose from the bourgeois decadence of the French *avant garde*.

If I mention Mr. Elliot especially in this connection, I am not of course forgetting such other notable knee-wives as Sir Stephen Tallents. I do so to illustrate the fact that, however differing the patterns of purpose may be, the common origin is forever a mighty consolidating form of communication. If he grasped the documentary potential quickly, I am sure it was for the selfsame reasons, direct and indirect, which had urged me to think about it. In the issue, whatever the diminishing returns might be in the grandiose use of the film to change the imaginative structure of our time, it meant that the documentary film, first of all the media ever to do so, found its basic economy in the Government service. It was soon on its way to serve the changing relationships of the Commonwealth, the changing relationships of Capital and Labour, the progressive development of the social services within the framework of social democracy and, ever more constantly, the scientific and technical education of our time.

To-day we can take its role in the more innocent spheres of information and persuasion for granted. The Government Departments are all using films nowadays as part and parcel of their necessary communication with the public. They use it to give an account of their stewardship or to secure public co-operation in enterprises of State. They use it to project the life of Britain and her Colonies to countries overseas and even to support the Nation's diplomatic representation in particular matters of international discussion : as, say, at the United Nations when affairs of Mandate or the treatment of backward peoples are under review. They use it to improve agricultural and industrial methods and to instruct the public in new patterns of local management and public health. In still more specialised ways, and at a hundred points, professional groups are advised of new discoveries and fresh techniques. The documentary use of the film is to-day, by and large, a normal and even ordinary tool of public information, guidance and persuasion : and so largely organised in production and distribution that, in the War period, it could quickly be mobilised into the most intensive of communication services.

Moreover, countries all across the world have followed Britain in this lead : to a point where one of the great developments is the exchange of these films between nation and nation on an ever increasing scale of specialised interest. To-day we make treaties between the nations for the exchange of films on all manner of scientific, technical, social and cultural levels. By films, we watch each other's achievements in medicine and child welfare, town planning and factory method, laboratory enquiry and aesthetic innovation; and there is hardly a nation from China to Peru which is not already involved, or becoming involved, in these State uses of the film which sprang from our simple notion. Indeed, paradoxically, the smaller nations are almost more concerned than the larger ones, if only because their place in the progressive world— yes, and their cultural defences against it—have the more firmly to be asserted.

Yet still I must return the analysis to its beginning. The older ones will surely follow me when I say that, though we may claim something for the progresive work of our generation in this as in other fields, larger powers, even more imaginatively directive of public event, were expected of the ideas we shared thirty years ago. The true mass educational potential of this documentary concept of ours has, in my view, scarcely been exercised. If we brought the working man in living terms to the screen and made a new art of observation in our tangled metropolitan world; if we joined its force gladly to the appreciation of social conditions and the clearance of the slums and did a little to stir the imagination to the brilliant new technical forces at men's command, we stopped short where the talents and persuasions of British social democracy stopped short. We did not tie this technical and creative force sufficiently and in time to the service of backward peoples nor indeed in this, as in other matters, to the great and even drastic educational task which has still somehow to be undertaken, if we are to bring to order the powerful issues which engage us. Let this be said for it, that we conceived from the first, and in this curious form, that the political task had its necessary counterpart in an educational task; and that this uniquely involved nothing less than a mass assault on the imagination through media capable of imaginative form. The problem is still there and the solution of it, at root, still to be developed. The fuller fruit of the documentary idea is therefore still to come. Come it will; for the onrush of events, the universal sense of impotence in regard to them and the patent sense of frustration in the creative arts, are alike the sign that the imaginative forces of order are not adequately deployed. Political forces must inevitably mature which will permit of that deployment.

EARNING BETWEEN LEARNING

By Alan C. Brown

Twenty-eight year old Alan C. Brown has travelled extensively at the expense of the Royal Corps of Signals in which he was a Corporal for five and a half years. Since his demobilisation in 1946 he has occupied his summers in a multitude of jobs and his winters in reading for a degree in Arts. Both occupations are an education as he shows in the following pages.

STUDENTS are proverbially short of cash—Scots students especially so. This worries them less than you might think and is a matter of pride to Scotsmen, reminding them as it does that throughout their history our Universities have exemplified that great and characteristic Scottish virtue, that lack of funds is no bar to learning.

Quite understandably, the " long vacation " is not a phrase that comes easily to Scottish lips. At no time during the last 500 years has any great proportion of Scots students been able to lie back and take their ease during the summer months.

For many there was the long walk back to the family croft where there was the urgent need of that additional pair of hands, spared during the winter months only by considerable sacrifice. For others there were the Parish schools waiting to be staffed.   The Education Act of 1696 reiterated the aim of the Reformers—a school in every Parish—and who better than the local youth studying Divinity at Glasgow to teach the children of the Parish the three R's and perhaps even a smattering of Latin? In this way, the student might earn enough from the Parish heritors and the pupil's nominal fees to see him through the winter at College and give him a few modest comforts in his city digs.

This was all very well in an 18th century Scotland that was four-fifths rural and in which most students were sons of the croft. In the 20th Century, however, students, like the rest of the population, are largely town dwellers. More of us live in towns in Scotland than in any other country in the world. Though students, therefore, still work during the holidays, only a few are now beckoned by a family croft.

Glasgow University students, last summer, could have been found in many diverse roles. Among these were conducting on Glasgow tramcars, sending out little buff income tax envelopes to their fellow citizens, running Housey-housey stalls at holiday fun fairs, wielding pick and shovel at Highland Hydro-electric schemes, acting as ward orderlies in city hospitals and chalking cues at Billy Butlin's billiard room at the Heads of Ayr. Women students were acting as benevolent nurses to families on holiday, serving behind counters in Glasgow bookshops and fashion stores and tidying rooms and making beds in coast hotels. Some students found their jobs by their own efforts, others were assisted by the Employment Committee of the Students' Representative Council.

Starting in 1947, the Employment Committee of the S.R.C. got fully under way in January, 1948 when they sent out over 300 circular letters to West of Scotland employers asking if they could make use of students' services during the summer and Christmas vacations. The result, as the Hollywood boys would say, was terrific, and several hundred students are now placed in jobs every year through the S.R.C. Many more, of course, find their own jobs and any attempt to quote figures would be the merest guesswork.

It may be of interest if I may say something about the different jobs I have tackled during my three years Arts course. Though I never attained any of the plums of student jobs like £10 a week in a Pollokshaws dyeworks or an equally fabulous sum as a Potato Inspector in Perthshire, the variety of my jobs has given me great scope for new experiences. In three years I have been a temporary postman, railway porter, agricultural labourer in the Swiss Alps, income tax clerk, tourist agents' courier, assistant purser on Clyde steamers and controller of crowds at a Sauchiehall Street store's January bargain sales for women. My experiences are only typical of hundreds of other students in most faculties.

I have never heard anyone suggest that vacational employment interferes with scholastic progress. My own feeling is that in helping to promote mental alertness by continual readjustment to different situations its effect is wholly beneficial. Merely to state the facts of my own case as relevant to the subject under consideration, I have never had any cause when exam results were announced to lament the time spent earning between learning.

Of all the holiday jobs I have tackled, pushing a barrow at Buchanan Street station was the one in which I was happiest. British Railways are a much maligned institution, but we can speak of an institution, as of a person, only as we find it. B.R. were, I found, a genial firm to work for. The experience was an education.

For example, I rather naively thought that if you are walking up the platform when a passenger asks you a question, you stop and answer. Nothing of the kind. To do this is only to encourage a veritable spate of questions. Your regular porter well knows that passengers always prepare their questions in a series of not less than four.

What you do in such a situation is slow down—that is quite permissible—and answer as you cruise past. This indicates . . . (a) that you are a busy man, and . . . (b) that platform indicators and station announcers supply all such information.

Since the days I clutched my spade and pail on the Gourock boat train, I have had the yearning to charge round a nicely packed railway station piloting one of these highly manoeuvrable four-wheeled bogeys. It was a great joy to me, therefore, to fulfil this boyhood urge and to be paid for doing so.

On my first day on duty with the barrow, however, passengers would not make a move to get out of my way, though repeatedly I asked to be excused in what I took to be a suitably stentorian manner. Happily, one of the regulars soon put me right.

What you do, of course, is jerk out " Mind your back! " and carry straight on regardless. A wide avenue is immediately opened up for you in that reverential way I thought Glasgow reserved only for Royalty.

At the first train I met, I was not hailed by a single passenger—a serious matter when a porter relies on his tips to bring his wage up to a comfortable round figure. Passengers stalked past me with their baggage, under the impression that I was there to meet a friend, and they would grab the next porter a few yards up the platform.

I soon discovered the explanation—I had no badge of office, i.e. a railway skip cap at the back of my head. Thanks to an understanding regular on the other shift, I was soon able to put that right. He lent me his cap, and from then on I was MADE.

By the end of the first week I had the job down to a fine art. I could handle awkward luggage and call taxis with such a polish that I have seen me coping with three different customers off the one train. Two shillings was quite a frequent tip, 2/6d. not unknown. The more hardened and seasoned type of traveller contented himself with something less, but it was all in the day's work.

One of the ex-Service students on duty with me had a rather bizarre experience. He told me that the first train he met had on board—of all people—the wife's sister. She was so obviously charmed by his thoughtfulness in coming to meet her, that he had not the heart to tell her that he was carrying her case in a professional capacity.

The relations between the regulars and student temporaries were excellent. The former looked on our amateurish and guileless ways with a kindly humanity. They took us under their wing and confided in us the secrets of their trade. When Glasgow returned from its holidays and the time came for British Railways and I to part, it was with a heavy heart that I left them.

It is only seldom now that I can afford to travel by rail, and on these rare occasions I can never afford to eat (luncheon minimum charge 5/-, coffee extra). Remembering my glorious hour with the B.R. barrow at Buchanan Street, however, I cannot find it in me to speak with anything but affection of my former employers.

My other holiday job with British Railways was as assistant purser on the Craigendoran steamers. I served chiefly on the "Lucy Ashton," that Grand Old Lady of the Clyde who was greatly mourned on her retiral from active service, particularly in newspaper offices throughout Scotland as Lucy could always be relied on to provide some interesting copy. You will remember, for example, how Lucy spurned the new coat of buff and black paint with which B.R. contrived to cover her familiar red, white and black N.B. colours. She, in turn, continually contrived to overheat her funnel so that the buff and black paint peeled off leaving her red, white and black coat in triumphant possession.

My duties on the Lucy were chiefly to make out cargo manifests, to stick charge labels on passengers' advanced luggage and to weigh consignments of returned empty crates which came aboard at Hunter's Quay and Kilcreggan. An important duty, too, was to arrange all the tickets in alphabetical and numerical order which passengers handed up at the gangway, bore a hole through the centre of the bundle and string all the tickets together. I never got to know the point of this intricate operation, but no doubt the officials up in Glasgow got a great deal of pleasure from the little bundles I used to send ashore every evening.

There came a time when I tired of the sea and resolved with two other Arts students to seek my fortune abroad before the new session started in October. A notice outside Pearce Lodge—S.R.C. H.Q.—told how one might earn money, meet students from many different lands and have a memorable holiday, all by attending one of the International Student Work Camps in Switzerland.

Wearing kilts, we set out at 7 o'clock one morning from a big road transport garage in Glasgow's Broomielaw to thumb our way to Switzerland. We made London in the early hours of the next day and were in Dover that evening. In six days we crossed France by lorry and private car from Dunkirk to Basle, meeting with many interesting experiences and much friendliness and hospitality en route.

12 nations—France, Belgium, Holland, Italy, Denmark, Switzerland, Germany, Austria, U.S.A., South Africa, England and Scotland—were represented at the work camp at which we finally checked in at Tambo high

up in the Swiss Alps near the Italian border. Language difficulties presented hardly any barrier, since the Danes, Germans and Swiss could speak English and we Glaswegians could endeavour to converse in French with the other Continentals.

At the outset, we received two big surprises—the work was much harder than we had expected and the pay much less. The work consisted of digging rocks out of the mountain side and rolling the boulders down the slopes, the idea being to make more pasturage for the mountain cattle. The opinion of the united nations, on this occasion unanimous, was that we might have worked there till doomsday without increasing to any notable degree the sustenance available for the cattle. Pay proved to be only a few shillings a week, after deduction of board and lodgings.

We were awakened each day except Sunday at 5 a.m. by a well-meaning, but, at that time in the morning, profoundly exasperating Swiss camp leader who came into the straw-lined disused farm building which was our billet, blowing a hunting horn. In a temperature that was never more than a few degrees above freezing point, we used to troop out and wash in a perishingly cold mountain stream which a few hundred feet higher up had been snow. At 5.30 a.m. we grabbed picks and shovels, round which a film of frost had formed during the night, and began work. At 7 a.m. there was a pause for breakfast— corn flakes, bread and jam—and, shortly after this, the sun would begin to appear over the mountains.

A revolutionary atmosphere began to pervade the camp, promoted in particular by the voluble and warmblooded Italians from the Sunny South who claimed to be slowly freezing to death and to have been much more comfortably off in a P.O.W. camp during the War. The German students worked away strenuously and unquestioningly, enjoying every minute of their activity and exuding the essence of courteousness to everyone.

We three Scots left after a fairly short stay, our chief difficulty being the lack of warm clothing, owing to the impossibility of carrying a wardrobe with us on a 1,000 mile Continental hitch-hike in the height of the summer. To be frank, too, the camp location and conditions were not just as we had visualized them from the notice outside Pearce Lodge or when chatting with the genial chap in the S.R.C. Employment Department.

I should like to tell you of my experiences at the Battle of the Sauchiehall Street sales and something of what I learned of human nature from behind the counter of an income tax office, but enough has perhaps been said to show that the educational opportunities of the 1951 Gilmorehill student are not necessarily confined to the lecture rooms and labs on that well-loved eminence.

GLASGOW UNIVERSITY ATHLETIC CLUB.
By W. R. CUNNINGHAM, M.A., LL.D.

For twenty-six years Dr. Cunningham has served the University as Librarian and keeper of the Hunterian books and manuscripts. He has also been a great friend to the student body. In this article he traces the history of the Athletic Club with which he has been associated for a generation.

ONE of the most striking features of the last eighty years has been the growth of organized sport. This is as true of University, as it is of national life. The origin of this movement may be taken as coinciding, roughly, with the removal to Gilmorehill from the Old College in the High Street in 1870. Of course the high spirits of youth had found vent in sports, pastimes and amusements since the beginning of time and certainly in the Old College down the centuries. The Old College Green had been the scene of football *en masse* and that combination of handball and football in hordes which continues to be played in some northern and border villages at New Year or on Shrove Tuesday. In his invaluable *Memories of the Old College of Glasgow* the late Dr. David Murray has reproduced from the *Illustrated London News* of 10th August, 1867, a picture of " Highland Games in the College Grounds, August, 1867." It might have been a prefiguration of the Braemar Gathering. But from the time of year and the universality of the kilt, I suspect that the picture implied nothing more than the loan of the College grounds to an outside body as in these days Westerlands is sometimes so lent during vacations; nor do I conclude that the accurate author himself meant more than this. He merely wished to give a good view of the environments of the Old College upon a romantic occasion. In the same volume Dr. Murray devotes some thirty pages to references to archery, golf, billiards (*globuli eburnei*) and fencing, amongst other sports. His descriptions and anecdotes are drawn from a wide variety of sources.

The Glasgow University Athletic Club was founded in 1881, and it assumed the management of the various sections of sport as they arose. In the beginning Rugby and Athletics were the only active sections, for the G.U.M., founded in 1889, had been in existence for some years before an Association section was organized. Now there are over twenty sections ranging from a most successful Boat Club to an equally successful Basketball Section.

Until 1908 the only ground at the disposal of the University, apart from fields occasionally rented for special purposes, was the space now occupied by the Zoology and Chemistry Buildings. In 1908 the Academicals had moved from Old Anniesland to New Anniesland. The University rented Old Anniesland, which at that time occupied about half the area now owned by the High School Club. Meanwhile Westerlands had been purchased and was steadily prepared for use. The various sections were moved thither after the 1914-18 war and the pavilion was opened by the late Lord Birkenhead at the Sports Day in 1925. Garscadden was subsequently acquired and opened by an impressive Field Day in 1936, when, appropriately enough, the first Rugby score was obtained by that accomplished footballer W. C. W. Murdoch, playing for a representative Glasgow team against the very powerful

University team of that year. The first " Soccer " goal was scored by the University playing against a combined Rangers-Celtic team.

Thanks to the generosity of the University Court, the supervision by the Management of Athletic Grounds Committee and the skill and loyalty of the head groundsmen and their wives, Westerland and Garscadden are models of what athletic grounds should be.

Although frequent complaints have been made about the lack of professorial support towards the Athletic Club, certain professors during the current century have not spared themselves in their devotions to the interests of the Club by acting as Honorary Presidents, presiding at meetings, and proving fertile in counsel. Professor D. J. Medley, the doyen of the *emeriti,* from shortly after his arrival in Glasgow in 1899 until the formation of the O.T.C. in 1909, when he directed his enthusiasm into hereditary military channels by becoming chairman of the Military Education Committee, did his utmost, by pen and voice, to maintain the highest standards. He constantly compared Glasgow achievements with those of Oxford and Cambridge, and tried to instil into students that high conception of loyalty to the University which would make them realise that during their sojourn at the University their main duty lay towards it and towards no other institution. He was succeeded by Professor F. O. Bower, that eminent mountaineer, whose vigour continued into a ripe old age. He in turn gave place for a year or so to Professor J. H. Teacher who never allowed his recognition of Academical qualities to divert him from service to the University. Then came Professor G. G. Henderson and the Very Reverend Professor Archibald Main, the latter runner-up in his youth to the accomplished C. C. Fitzgerald in the 440 yards. Professor Main in the Athletic Club Jubilee Year of 1931 pleaded eloquently for more support from teaching staff and students. Then came Professor C. A. Campbell, still happily with us, whose skill in Rugby, Lawn Tennis and Badminton and whose faculty of leading young men made him the ideal Honorary President. To these names I would add that of the late Roy Young, for 18 years the President of the Rugby Club. His knowledge, quiet strength and pervasive influence were a powerful factor in the success of the Rugby Club when it was at the pinnacle of its achievement.

As student presidents hold office normally for one year they are rather numerous and my selection of names may appear somewhat arbitrary. C. F. P. Fraser (1885-89) was a Scottish Rugby Internationalist as was A. M. Stevenson (1908-09). C. C. Fitzgerald (1904-05) and H. G. Wilson (1907-08 and 1910-11) were Irish Rugby Internationalists, the latter one of the great forwards of all time. G. Stewart (1901-02) beat W. H. Welsh of Edinburgh in the 100 yards, edited the G.U.M., took a First in History and died in action in 1916. A. R. Forrester (1923-24) was eminent in Rugby, Cricket and Lawn Tennis. G. P. Richardson (1931-32), an excellent high jumper, continues to serve the Club as Manager of Athletic Grounds. T. H. Souter (1933-34), a splendid stand-off, won the 440 yards Hurdles and was an Amateur Soccer Internationalist. R. N. M. Robertson, long record-holder in the Broad Jump, a Scottish champion for three years, an Inter-city player and International reserve wing three-quarter, H. M. Murray (1936-37), an International centre three-quarter and an Inter-University and Scottish Champion quarter miler, J. A. M. Robertson (1941-42), for some years holder of the best performances at Westerlands in 220, 440 and 880 yards, the supreme stylist, and R. F. Edington (1949-50), Inter-University and Scottish champion pole-vaulter—all these were men of mark. Two others I should mention apart, R. S. Sloan (1945-46), whom cruel illness

M

struck down in the year of his presidency and caused to abandon the game of Rugby in which he excelled, but who since that time has not failed in his devotion to the Club, and Ian N. Lapraik (1939-40), three miler and cross-country runner, who in three short years or so passed from Cadet to Lieutenant-Colonel (Acting Brigadier), saw service in aeroplanes and submarines, and finished with D.S.O., O.B.E., M.C., not to mention foreign decorations.

At Oxford and Cambridge the award of a " Blue " is an honour as keenly sought and as highly prized as an international cap. If all students at Glasgow did what ought to be an elementary duty and played for the University in the Sport in which they are expert, Glasgow would be as supreme in various branches as she is at the moment in the province of pure athletics. In her athletic team this year she counted the following past or present Scottish champions :—R. M. Ward (100 yards), D. K. Gracie (440 yards), T. B. Begg (880 yards), G. Muir Fraser and R. H. Boyd (440 yards Hurdles), S. O. Williams (Broad Jump), J. E. F. Clarke (Javelin) and R. F. Edington (Pole Vault), surely an unrivalled assembly of champions from one club. In addition the Relay Team hold the Scottish Mile Medley Championship and set up the record of 3 minutes 31.7 seconds for the distance. If there is any particular distance at which our athletes seem to excel it is that beautiful and most punishing race, the 440 yards, and one recalls the names of J. B. Bell, J. G. McColl, J. N. Miller, I. H. Borland, H. M. Murray, W. M. O. Rennie, W. D. H. Conacher and D. K. Gracie, all of them Scottish champions since 1919, although the two last mentioned did not gain their championships whilst matriculated students. Nor must the name of Robin Murdoch be omitted from any survey of Glasgow University athletes. President of the Union, good wing three-quarter and Scottish champion over the 100 and 220 yards, he is

the only Glasgow University athlete ever to secure the
signal distinction of an A.A.A. Championship (220 yards)
and that on two occasions. Nor in athletics must the
achievements of women students be forgotten—in the
High Jump Miss E. D. Cathcart and Miss D. Walby, in
the Broad Jump Miss May J. Baird, in the 100 and 220
Miss Betty Miller and Miss Maureen Malcolm, in the 440
Miss M. D. Rae and Miss A. A. Livingston, in the 80
metres hurdles Miss Doris Young and Miss E. Unkles, and
in the Javelin and Discuss Miss Betty McInnes. Names
crowd to memory thick and fast—in Rugby, Adam Brown,
Teddy Maitland, Sandy Miller, Hugh McLaren, T. M.
Hart (2 caps) and H. S. Mackintosh (16 caps); in swim-
ming, M. R. Chassels, Trevor Harrop and Miss Nora
Yates; in Water Polo, R. R. McGarvey; in lawn tennis,
C. R. Marks and J. G. Rutherglen; in boxing, Herbert
Brash and W. E. Watson; in Hockey, H. J. Hunter Boyd,
G. S. Milne, D. R. Sloan and J. F. Cowper; in Women's
Hockey, the internationalists Misses I. Hutchinson, M. M.
King and K. MacGregor; in Badminton E. B. (now Sir
Eric) Bowyer, A. M. O. Dobbie, J. Cameron Love and
R. R. Macdonald, Misses A. M. Gilzean, Sheila Dobbie
and M. B. Forrester; in Golf, S. L. McKinlay, R. R. Jack
and F. W. G. Deighton; in Women's Golf, Miss S.
Conacher and Miss G. Galbraith; in cricket, D. Burnett,
H. F. Sheppard and R. O. MacKenna; in the more recent
sport of Fencing, A. H. Stenning, J. Fleck and J. A. C.
Ferguson and Misses C. L. H. Noble and J. M. S.
Armstrong; and in Association football J. F. Orr and C.
M. Maclean. Amongst all-rounders there are, within the
Athletic Section, the incomparable A. N. Lapsley (Scottish
champion in High Jump and Javelin and long the record
holder in the Hammer and a good performer in Broad
Jump, Hurdles and Putt); J. H. Schneiderman, American
expert in Field Events, especially the Discus, and Bill
McNeish who with performances in Hammer (Record),

Putt, Discus and Pole Vault helped in large measure to win this year's Inter-Varsity Sports. In different sports N. A. Selkirk—killed in action—(Rugby, Hurdles and Lawn Tennis), W. E. C. Taylor (Hockey, Cricket, Fives, Badminton, Athletics), W. W. Weir (Rugby, Cricket, Billiards, Lawn Tennis), and G. R. Roxburgh (Rugby, Fives, Lawn Tennis) are striking examples of varied accomplishment.

Anxious students may be assured that the highest achievements in the field of sport are not incompatible with the highest academic success. Miss Jean C. Rankine had a large number of Hockey Caps, she was Lawn Tennis Champion of Scotland, she had First Class Honours in Mathematics, and she was a lecturer in that subject at the University. Dr. R. A. Robb, senior Lecturer in Mathematics, was Scottish 100 yards champion, gives valuable instruction to our runners and is Chairman of the Management of Athletic Grounds Committee. T. B. Begg last session played wing three-quarter for the XV, won the Scottish Inter-Varsity 880 yards in record time, won the Scottish championship at that distance and gained the Brunton Memorial Prize as the best medical Graduate of 1950.

And what is the popular view of the relative value of sporting and academic successes? Lord Loreburn, Cheltenham and Balliol, Lord Chancellor of Great Britain in the administrations of Campbell-Bannerman and Asquith, remarked, somewhat ruefully, to a friend—" In my early days at the Bar many a solicitor's clerk bringing me a brief would ask ' Are you the Mr. Reid who kept wicket for Oxford? ' Never a one asked ' Are you the Mr. Reid who won the Ireland? ' " And perhaps even here it should be added for information that the Ireland Scholarship is the chief prize for classical scholarship at Oxford.

UNIVERSITY OF GLASGOW
STUDENTS' FIFTH CENTENARY COMMITTEE

The Committee was elected in two parts: on the 6th May, 1948, and on the 19th January, 1950, when it was found necessary to enlarge the representation.

1948

Convener—

Donald Macmillan	S.R.C.
Miss Elspeth Gallie	S.R.C.
James Lawrie	G.U. Union
Pamela Gibson	Q.M. Union
A. R. Pate	G.U.A.C.
Sir Frederick Stewart, LL.D.	Rector's Assessor
Professor J. Fordyce, M.A.	Clerk of Senate
Rev. A. M. L. MacFarlane, M.C.	Pres. S.R.C.

Minutes Secy.—

Mrs. J. Hunter	Clerk of Council

1950

Convener—

Donald Macmillan	S.R.C.
*Dorothy Little, M.A.	S.R.C.
David J. Mackay	Pres. S.R.C.

A. George King	Pres. G.U. Union 1949-50
W. G. A. Craig, M.A.	Pres. G.U. Union 1950-51
James Lawrie	G.U. Union
Jean Geddes, M.A.	Pres. Q.M. Union 1949-50
Stroma Duncan, M.A.	Pres. Q.M. Union 1950-51.
Pamela Gibson	Q.M. Union
R. F. Edington, M.B., CH.B.	Pres. G.U.A.C. 1949-50
David Johnstone, M.C., M.A.	Pres. G.U.A.C. 1950-51
A. R. Pate	G.U.A.C.

Court—

R. T. Hutcheson, Esq., M.A., PH.D.	Secretary

Senate—

Professor C. J. Fordyce, M.A.	Clerk of Senate

Elected Members—

J. J. Tennyson-d'Eyncourt	Ball
Gerald A. Fisher	Co-ordinating
George S. Riddell	Entertainments
William G. Burnside	Finance
William A. Dunsmuir, M.A.	Hospitality
Thomas H. Shanks	Other Functions
Alastair G. Ramsay	Procession
*Ian W. Nicholson Duncan R. Robertson	Publicity
Ian R. Hamilton	Editor, Commemoration Volume

In Attendance—
    William Adams, B.L.   Manager, Royal
                                        Bank of Scotland,
                                        Charing Cross

Minutes Secretary—
    Miss A. M. H. Sutherland

* Note (1)—Miss Florence Ferguson, M.A., President
Q.M. section S.R.C., became a member of
Committee *vice* Miss Dorothy Little, M.A.,
who retired from Council October 1950,
and Mr. Thomas Colvin, B.Sc., Vice-President S.R.C., was appointed since the
Convener was also President S.R.C.

* Note (2)—Ian Nicholson was called to the Forces in
August 1950 and Duncan R. Robertson was
appointed by the Committee.

* Note (3)—Sir Frederick Stewart died in April 1950.